THE BRITISH EMPIRE
and Queen Victoria
in World History

Catherine Bernard

Enslow Publishers, Inc.

40 Industrial Road   PO Box 38
Box 398   Aldershot
Berkeley Heights, NJ 07922   Hants GU12 6BP
USA   UK

http://www.enslow.com

In loving memory of my grandmother, Helen McManus Bernard

Library of Congress Cataloging-in-Publication Data

Bernard, Catherine.
     The British Empire and Queen Victoria in world history / Catherine
Bernard.
          p. cm. — (In world history)
Summary: Explores the rule of Queen Victoria, the longest-reigning
British monarch, who brought Great Britain to the height of its power,
building a great colonial empire while enjoying industrial expansion at
home.
Includes bibliographical references (p.) and index.
     ISBN 0-7660-1824-5
     1. Great Britain—Colonies—History—19th century—Juvenile
literature. 2. Great Britain—History—Victoria, 1837–1901—Juvenile
literature. 3. Victoria, Queen of Great Britain, 1819–1901—Juvenile
literature. [1. Great Britain—History—Victoria, 1837–1901. 2. Great
Britain—Colonies—History—19th century. 3. Victoria, Queen of Great
Britain, 1819-1901. 4. Kings, queens, rulers, etc.] I. Title. II.
Series.
DA16 .B39 2002
941.081—dc21

                              2002003972

Printed in the United States of America

10 9 8 7 6 5 4 3 2 1

To Our Readers:
We have done our best to make sure all Internet Addresses in this book were
active and appropriate when we went to press. However, the author and the
publisher have no control over and assume no liability for the material available
on those Internet sites or on other Web sites they may link to. Any comments or
suggestions can be sent by e-mail to comments@enslow.com or to the address on
the back cover.

Illustration Credits: Charles Hogarth, *Illustrations of World-Famous
Places* (New York: Dover Publications, Inc., 1993), p. 4; Enslow
Publishers, Inc., pp. 22, 74, 94; Reproduced from the Collections of the
Library of Congress, pp. 11, 28, 31, 35, 42, 48, 51, 61, 65, 70, 72, 81, 83,
87, 90, 96, 106, 108, 111.

Cover Illustration: © Digital Vision Ltd. All Rights Reserved
(Background); Reproduced from the Collections of the Library of
Congress (Queen Victoria portrait).

Contents

Queen Victoria's Golden Jubilee took place in Westminster Abbey, a world-famous church in London, England.

Chapter 1

The Golden Jubilee

On the morning of June 21, 1887, nearly half a million people lined the streets of London, England.[1] Military guards in full uniform gathered on horseback in front of Buckingham Palace, where Queen Victoria lived. Marching bands played and onlookers cheered all along the parade route, which would end at Westminster Abbey. All were there to celebrate the great Golden Jubilee—the fiftieth anniversary of the queen coming to the throne.

Much had changed in the fifty years that Victoria had ruled over England and its empire. The tiny old woman was certainly no longer the eighteen-year-old girl she was when she was crowned in 1837. In fact, while the sixty-eight-year-old queen enjoyed the Jubilee festivities, she was completely exhausted by day's end. Later that night she wrote in her journal:

I was half dead with fatigue, and after sitting down a moment with Marie of Belgium, slipped away and was rolled back to my room . . . to try and see something of the very general illuminations, but could not see much. The noise of the crowd, which began yesterday, went on till late. Felt truly grateful that all had passed off so admirably and this never-to-be-forgotten day will always leave the most gratifying and heart-stirring memories behind.[2]

Her energy level was not the only trait that had changed. Nine children and a taste for good food made the barely five-foot-tall monarch seem nearly as wide as she was tall.[3] Unlike fashionable women of late-nineteenth-century England, Victoria preferred the style of dress from twenty years earlier. And, as always, she wore only black as a sign of her constant mourning for the death of her beloved husband, Albert. He had died two decades earlier in 1861. Victoria's small stature and her old-fashioned dress made her seem more like a quaint doll than the ruler of the world's largest empire.

Like the queen, the landscape of the country she ruled over had changed over the last half century. In 1830, seven years before Victoria was crowned, one of the most important and technologically advanced railways in the world had been built to connect the cities of Liverpool and Manchester. By the year of the Golden Jubilee, even small rural towns were linked by a growing network of railroads. The miles of rail line in the country nearly doubled, from 6,621 to 11,789, between 1850 and 1875 alone.[4] The new railway lines in turn led to booms in the coal and iron industries as well.

Increasing industrialization was also reflected in other areas. Great advances in technology—known collectively as the Industrial Revolution—completely transformed the way people worked and lived. In the textile industry—the production of cloth—for example, new technology replaced handlooms with mass factory production. Hundreds of workers moved from rural areas to big cities in the hopes of finding factory work. As a result, the social, economic, and cultural landscape of the entire country changed.

Of course, the British Industrial Revolution was not without cost. Cities grew increasingly over-crowded. Uneven distribution of wealth allowed only a small portion of society to grow rich. At the same time, the exploding population of poor was forced to live and work in horrible conditions. As a result of these inequities, Victoria's reign saw the rise of many organized political movements aimed at improving living and working conditions for the working class. Mid- to late-nineteenth-century England was a period of other wide-ranging social reform movements— from education reform to the women's rights movement, from political reform to the protection against cruelty to animals.

Exciting as the national transformations must have been, perhaps the greatest changes during Victoria's reign occurred with the expansion of the British Empire abroad. During her sixty-four years on the throne, eighteen major territories and many other minor ones were added to the empire. The practice of one nation or government forcibly extending its rule over another is known as imperialism. Many countries took part in imperialism in the nineteenth century, including France, Germany, Italy, and Spain. Britain, though, extended its influence farther than any other country. By the end of the nineteenth century, one quarter of the world's population were subjects of Queen Victoria.[5]

British territories included white settlement colonies such as Canada and Australia and important trade ports such as Hong Kong and Singapore. Other colonies, like India, offered profitable raw materials and export possibilities. They also provided employment opportunities for middle-class British men who wanted to work abroad. Still other territories, especially many in Africa, were colonized simply to keep other European nations from doing the same.

The expansion of the British Empire proved extremely profitable for the motherland. Imports and exports of all British territories were valued at approximately 117 million British pounds in 1830. By 1900, the sum grew to an unprecedented 878 million pounds.[6] Some of this wealth was invested back into the colonies to develop public works and resources such as roads, telegraph wires, bridges, railways, and schools. Most of these enhancements, though, were intended for Britain to use and benefit from. For the most part, the money went back into the pocket

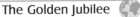

of the empire and very little trickled down to the colonized people themselves. The colonized also saw their land, culture, religion, and even language taken over by the self-proclaimed superior British.

For the people of Britain, the empire was not only a source of wealth, but a source of great pride as well. Over the course of her reign, Victoria saw popular enthusiasm for Britain's world dominance increase dramatically. As symbolic head of the empire, Victoria saw her own popularity as monarch grow as well. In cheering wildly for Queen Victoria that June morning, the British people were not merely celebrating their queen, they were celebrating the vast empire the doll-like old woman had come to represent.

The Life of a Queen-to-Be

Alexandrina Victoria was born May 24, 1819. Although she would one day be the reigning queen of the world's largest empire, her unimpressive birth did not foreshadow that fact. Victoria, or Drina, as she was known as a small child, was born a relatively poor relation of an argumentative royal family. Her mother, the Duchess of Kent, underwent a very dangerous journey from Germany where she was living, just so her daughter could be born on British soil. Because she and her husband, the Duke of Kent, were always in debt, they were forced to borrow money to pay for the trip.

The early 1800s was not a good time for the British royal family. Public opinion of the monarchy was very low. Internal family arguments also made for an extremely tense atmosphere. Victoria's paternal

King George III, Victoria's grandfather, cast a shadow on the British monarchy that took decades to reverse.

grandfather was King George III. George III was as famous for losing the American colonies during the American Revolution as he was for going mad by the end of his reign. George's embarrassing loss and his insanity caused the British people much alarm about other members of his royal family. They did not know if George's heirs would be better able to rule the British Empire. They also worried that his relatives could one day go insane, too. Before Victoria became queen, it was unclear if Britain would ever feel comfortable with its monarch again.

George III's death in 1820 was cause for only partial celebration. His equally unpopular son George IV succeeded him. King George IV was an unpleasant man who came to represent both the showiness and the unnecessary excesses of the British monarchy. In addition to heavy spending, he was known for extravagant tastes in food. Decades of eating rich food and drinking the best wines made him grow so enormous that it took his dressers hours to stuff him into his royal clothes.[1] George IV and his wife had only one daughter, Charlotte, who died in childbirth in 1817. The king had no heir to whom he could pass the crown. Next in line was the king's brother William, also childless. William was followed by another brother, Edward Duke of Kent, Victoria's father.

The irritable king hated his brother Edward in particular because he thought him frivolous and irresponsible with money. The king was quite right in this last impression, as the duke and duchess were indeed constantly in debt. The duchess in particular was constantly asking her wealthier relatives for a larger monthly allowance. Her nagging only gave the king more reason to dislike his brother's family. The Duke of Kent died suddenly from complications of a common cold just seven months after Victoria was born. Much as the king disliked his brother, he could not help but admit the importance of this timely birth. Should he and his brother William remain childless, Victoria would become queen upon their deaths.

Early Years at Kensington

Despite her royal status, Victoria grew up living in a set of run-down apartments in the relatively dingy Kensington Palace. Other members of the royal family, including the king, lived at the much more glamorous Windsor Castle. Although the little girl knew nothing of her surroundings, Victoria's mother was very aware of the family's financial situation. The family was in such debt that the duchess could not afford to return to London after her husband's death. As would often prove the case, the duchess depended on the generosity of her brother, Prince Leopold, the future king of Belgium. Leopold was the widowed husband of King George IV's dead daughter, Charlotte. The Duchess of Kent loved her daughter greatly, but she also recognized, and perhaps exploited, the political possibilities Victoria's position could offer. The duchess used this leverage in dealing

Source Document

My earliest recollections are connected with Kensington Palace, where I can remember crawling on a yellow carpet spread out for that purpose. . . . I was brought up very simply—never had a room to myself till I was nearly grown up—always slept in my Mother's room till I came to the Throne. . . . I sat and took my lessons in my Governess's bedroom. I was not fond of learning as a little child—and baffled every attempt to teach me my letters up to 5 years old—when I consented to learn them by their being written down before me.[2]

A fifty-three-year-old Victoria recorded the above memories of her childhood in her diary in 1872.

with not only King Leopold, but King George IV as well.

Another member of the Kensington Palace household who hoped his relationship to Victoria could improve his own social standing was Irishman John Conroy, the duchess's personal secretary. Conroy was also widely rumored to be the duchess's lover after her husband's death, although this has never been confirmed. Like the duchess, Conroy was very ambitious. He hoped Victoria could eventually propel him into a position of greater importance. Ultimately, he hoped to be the queen's personal secretary, an extremely influential position within the monarchy. Often in partnership with the duchess, Conroy plotted to influence Victoria. He wanted to ensure that he would have the best possible position if and when the little girl became queen. Victoria was a very clever girl, however. As she grew older, she became increasingly wary of Conroy's questionable ways.

While the duchess and Conroy were angling for more money and power, Victoria lived unaware of her family's financial status during her very early years. Victoria would play in the gardens or ride the pony that her uncle gave her as a gift. Before Victoria turned nine, her half sister Feodora (the duchess's daughter from a previous marriage) would keep her company. After Feodora was married to a German nobleman, Victoria had only Conroy's daughter Victoire to play with. Victoria disliked Conroy's daughter very much, though, and chose not to spend much time with her.

Perhaps to make up for having so few playmates, Victoria took to playing with dolls. She would make and dress the dolls herself, with the help of her governess, Louise Lehzen. Lehzen was another important and influential person in Victoria's childhood. Together they created careful records of the doll's names. They also invented personality traits for each of the 132 dolls in Victoria's collection.[3] The dolls and the fantasy worlds Victoria created for them provided the young girl with the companions she was otherwise lacking. She continued to play with them often, through the age of fourteen.

While she enjoyed her leisure time, Victoria was not as fond of her studies. She was a somewhat rebellious child and refused to learn the letters of the alphabet until she was five years old. Lehzen, as the princess's governess, taught her history, geography, and mathematics. Victoria felt she was quite good at math in particular. Victoria also had foreign language tutors to teach her French and German. As a member of the royal family, it was also important for Victoria to learn to be "a proper lady." For this reason, she also had lessons in dancing, singing, and drawing.

In addition to her lessons, Victoria spent a large portion of her time writing. She corresponded often with her Uncle Leopold. He offered her much-needed advice and guidance as she grew older. Victoria also began keeping a journal, which she wrote in almost every day of her adolescent and adult life.

Closer to the Throne

After years of shunning his widowed sister-in-law and her daughter, King George IV realized he could ignore them no longer. It was clear that he and his wife were past their childbearing years. Likewise, his aging brother William and his wife, who had watched their two infant children die, were not likely to have more.

It was looking more and more as if Victoria would be queen. While he still disliked the duchess, the king invited the family to Windsor Palace in 1826 for the first time. If nothing else, perhaps he was hoping to lessen the duchess's influence over the young girl. Victoria liked her "Uncle King" very much. She was quite proud of the diamond brooch he gave her that afternoon.[4] Despite other invitations to the palace, the king's opportunity to influence Victoria was ultimately rather short-lived. He died in June 1830. As William took his brother's place as king, Victoria was only one step from the throne.

Poor William, however, was not a typical king. Unlike his brother, he never expected to be king and was therefore never groomed for it. He had spent his youth drinking and having affairs with many women. William was the father of literally dozens of illegitimate children across the country. William did not care for the refined royal life. He was prone to wild outbursts and mood swings. His less-than-royal behavior did little to improve the public image of the monarchy.

King William was already sixty-five when he was crowned. He was asthmatic, overweight, and in generally poor health from his years of heavy drinking. If he were to die before Victoria turned eighteen, a regent—someone who rules in place of another— would be appointed to rule for her. By an order of Parliament, that regent would be Victoria's mother.

When the duchess recognized the possibility that she might temporarily rule the country, her demands became even more unbearable. While William may have been very different from his older, more refined brother, he did have one characteristic in common with him—an extreme dislike of the Duchess of Kent. He vowed to stay alive to see his niece turn of age and rightfully take the crown.

For a short time, it did not look like Victoria would have the chance to become queen anyway. In 1835, in her sixteenth year, she became quite ill. After months of battling fatigue, joint pain, and finally fever, she was diagnosed with typhoid, a serious disease that often proved fatal. As Lehzen tried to nurse her mistress back to health, the duchess and Conroy wondered what would become of them if Victoria died. Conroy decided to take matters into his own hands. He tried to force Victoria to sign a letter legally securing him a place as private secretary should she become queen. He even enlisted the duchess to persuade her daughter to sign the document. Despite her fever, Victoria managed to ward off Conroy's aggressive attempts. Eventually, she recovered fully from her illness. She did not forget what Conroy had tried to do. She distrusted him completely from that day on. Victoria was also saddened by her mother's role in Conroy's plan. She felt their relationship was always somewhat strained afterward.

Victoria was not the only one who recognized the inappropriateness of the duchess's and Conroy's behavior. King William was very upset and chose to make his feelings public at his 1836 birthday celebration. In front of hundreds of guests, he proclaimed the following:

> I trust in God that my life may be spared for nine months longer, after which period, in the event of my death no regency would take place. I should then have the satisfaction of leaving the royal authority to the personal exercise of that young lady [pointing to Victoria], the heiress presumptive to the crown, and not in the hands of a person now near me, who is surrounded by evil advisers and who is herself incompetent to act with propriety in the station in which she would be placed.[5]

Everyone in attendance knew immediately that the king was speaking of his sister-in-law and Conroy. The duchess turned bright red and Victoria burst into tears. It seemed her transition to queen would not be a smooth one.

A New Queen

May 24, 1837, Victoria's eighteenth birthday, came and went without event. The king was not well, though. It was doubtful he would live much longer. Less than a month later, early in the morning on June 20, King William died.

Only a few hours later, officials from Windsor Palace were sent to tell Victoria the news.

> I was awoke at 6 o'clock by Mamma, who told me that the Archbishop of Canterbury and Lord Conyngham were here, and wished to see me. I got out of bed and went into my sitting-room (only in my dressing-gown), and alone, and saw them. Lord Conyngham then acquainted me that my poor Uncle, the King, was no

more, and had expired at 12 minutes [past] 2 this morning, and consequently that I am Queen.[6]

It was an emotional day for Victoria. While she was no doubt excited to hear that she was queen, she was also grieving the death of her uncle at the same time. One person who helped her greatly was the prime minister, William Lamb, Lord Melbourne. With his aid, Victoria rehearsed the proclamation speech she would give later that morning, before receiving oaths of allegiance from her counselors.

Though barely eighteen, Victoria took on her new position with a surprising amount of poise and dignity. In only her first few hours as queen, she seemed to command greater respect than George III, George IV, or William had before her. Even so, the public still wondered if Victoria would be able to reverse the negative image of the British monarchy. England and the world at large were waiting to see what kind of ruler she would be. Making these expectations even more challenging to live up to was the time period itself. Victoria came to the throne at a time when her country and her empire were in the process of changing on many fronts right before her eyes.

Chapter 3

The British Empire

Victoria's coronation that day in 1837 marked the beginning of what would be a sixty-four-year reign—the longest in British history. Enormous changes would take place during that time period, from increased industrialization, to technological innovations, to an expanded empire. The sixty-plus years of Victoria's reign, though, were greatly influenced by the long and complex history of the empire that came before her.

The First Empire

Explorers such as John Cabot sailed under the English flag as early as 1451. The British Empire's aggressive colonization of land abroad, however, did not really begin until the sixteenth century, during Queen Elizabeth I's reign. From 1558 to 1603, England

Under the reign of Queen Elizabeth I, Britain began to colonize North America.

explored and began to colonize the eastern coast of North America. The English established trading companies in the East Indies, Turkey, and Russia. At the end of Elizabeth's reign, Ulster in Ireland—most of which is today Northern Ireland—was also made subject to the British flag, after a series of long and hostile wars.

In the seventeenth century, England's foreign policy became more clearly focused on imperialism— the process of expanding a nation's power by gaining control and influence over other areas. Much of the motivation to expand came from competition with European rivals such as France, Spain, Holland, and Portugal for profitable resources and markets abroad. The imperial drive during the First Empire was essentially motivated by mercantilism—economic policies developed to increase the power and wealth of a nation.

Establishing colonies loyal to the motherland allowed a country to create trade monopolies— exclusive control of the buying and selling of goods and services in a particular area. Establishing a colony meant the mother country would always have a place to sell the products it manufactured at home. In addition, colonies provided the mother country with valuable raw resources not available in England, such as sugar, tobacco, and dyes. These resources could then be harvested and sold for profit. England protected its new trade markets by passing several Navigation Acts throughout the century to limit foreign countries' ability to trade with British colonies. These acts ensured that the greatest possible profit would be returned to England.

Britain focused much of its initial imperialist attention on North America. Other countries, including Holland, France, and Spain, were also interested in North American land. By 1670, there were British American colonies in Massachusetts, Pennsylvania, Virginia, and Maryland, and settlements in the Bermudas, Honduras, Antigua, Barbados, and Nova Scotia. The northern half of the continent provided England with money from the fur trade. Sugar and tobacco cultivation offered profits from the southern half. Despite the presence of native peoples on the continent, Britain considered the land uninhabited and therefore used it to establish settlements as well. American Indians were forced westward as Britain developed its colonies along the east coast.

Other territories colonized during the seventeenth century included areas in the Eastern Hemisphere. India, for example, offered valuable spices and other natural resources. In addition, the western and northern regions of Africa were used to acquire slaves. In the eighteenth century, the buying and selling of slaves played a large role in the economic growth of Britain's North American colonies. The slaves were used in Britain's American and Caribbean colonies primarily as a source of labor for large farms and plantations. England was later one of the first countries to outlaw the slave trade, in 1807, although slavery itself was not abolished in the British colonies until 1833.

Imperial Wars

Throughout the eighteenth century, England's hold on North America was threatened by other countries, particularly by France. England and France were bitter enemies. The two countries had been fighting in North America since 1689. Fighting began once again as early as 1754. By 1756, the two countries were officially involved in what would become known as the Seven Years' War. (The Seven Years' War was simultaneously being fought in Europe between other major European countries, including Austria, Russia, Sweden, and Prussia, which is today part of Germany.) England was ultimately victorious over France on the North American front, which was called the French and Indian War. In 1763, the Treaty of Paris was signed, granting England virtually all of France's North American possessions. The treaty also excluded France from continuing its imperialist activities in India.

On one hand, England's defeat of France seemed to establish the country as the leading power in North America. At the same time, 1763 signaled a turning point in Britain's governance of its colonies on that continent. These changes would eventually have a major impact on the First Empire.

The presence of France in North America prior to 1763 had encouraged American colonists to be

25

particularly loyal to mother England. American colonists feared a French invasion and looked to Britain to protect them. Once that fear was removed, the colonies grew more confident in challenging Britain's authority. Simultaneously, Britain wanted to have more control over its colonies after the Seven Years' War. Britain's increased control made many colonists unhappy. Perhaps the victory over France made Britain overly confident that it was an uncontested superpower. If a country as powerful as France could not defeat Britain, many thought a smaller, less organized group of colonies could not pose any real threat to the empire.

In part, this kind of thinking led Britain to move ahead with its new policies. Britain changed aspects of the government and rewrote taxation laws, largely without consulting its colonies. Most Americans resented these threats to their liberties. They grew increasingly unhappy with British policies such as "taxation without representation." Under this policy, the colonists were forced to pay money to Britain without having representation in Parliament, Britain's governing body. By 1776, the colonies declared war and the American Revolution was officially under way. The war lasted seven years, with America ultimately winning its independence from Britain.

Another Treaty of Paris was signed in 1783. It recognized the independence of the United States of America. Ironically, while the first Treaty of Paris increased the size of the British Empire, the second treaty, signed only twenty years later, represented the country's first major colonial loss. In fact, Britain even lost some of the territory it had gained from France in 1763. The end of the American Revolution effectively signaled the end of the First British Empire.

The Second Empire

What is known as the Second British Empire began expanding almost immediately after the decline of the first. As many as one hundred thousand Loyalists—the American colonists who had remained loyal to Britain during the American Revolution—found themselves without a country at the war's end.[1] The majority emigrated to Canada, creating large British colonies there in the process. Other Loyalists established new settlements in the Caribbean.

Yet another series of wars with the French, the Napoleonic Wars, also increased the size of the Second Empire. Under the command of famous general Napoleon Bonaparte, the French attempted to put an end to Britain's dominance of trade. The British officially declared war in 1806. They fought until they once again defeated the French forces, this time at the Battle of Waterloo, in present-day Belgium, in 1815. With Napoleon's defeat, the British gained territories as far ranging as South Africa, Ceylon (an island, known today as Sri Lanka, off the coast of India), Trinidad, and a handful of other Caribbean islands.

This cartoon highlights the animosity between Britain and France during the Napoleonic Wars. In it, a rather large Englishman is gobbling up a tiny French soldier.

The British Empire continued to grow greatly in the Eastern Hemisphere as well as in the Western Hemisphere. The British East India Company had controlled coastal parts of India, for example, since 1600. The East India Company began as a purely commercial agency. It gradually evolved into an administrative agency controlled directly by the British government. By the early nineteenth century, British control extended from the coast to central India.

As Southeast Asia became more important in terms of strategic bases and trade routes, Britain also looked to control other land in the area. Sir Thomas Stamford Raffles focused on the small island of Singapore, which could serve as a valuable seaport. Raffles encouraged the British to take over the island. By 1816, it, too, was under British rule. Another British holding, Australia, was originally used as a penal colony—a prison—for British convicts. The first prisoners arrived in 1788 at Botany Bay. By the early nineteenth century, several other penal colonies were established, as well as some territories for free settlers.

Industrial Revolution

Geography was not the only aspect of the British Empire to change during the years before Victoria's reign. Major economic and technological transformations, known collectively as the Industrial Revolution, were altering the face of the world at a very fast pace.

England had already established itself far and away as the most industrialized country in the world well before the time Victoria took the throne. There were several factors that made this possible. First, the country was rich in important natural resources such as coal and iron. Geographically, its waterways and coastlines were easy to navigate and therefore favorable for trade. Ideas and knowledge, particularly in science and technology, were widely shared, creating an atmosphere where invention was encouraged and nurtured.

As early as 1780, advanced industrialization allowed Britain to produce more goods at a faster rate than ever before. The first industry to be transformed by the Industrial Revolution was the textile industry. Textiles refer to the production of cloth made from raw material such as cotton. In fact, the change to mechanical production in this industry was so successful that cotton textiles accounted for an unprecedented 40 percent of British exports by 1815.[2] James Watt's invention of an improved steam engine in 1769 changed the power source for most factories. New machinery meant weaving could be done quickly on power looms instead of by hand. This new machinery in turn increased the demand for iron and coal, two industries growing in their own right. Conditions such as weather and daylight no longer dictated when work could be done. Work on machines could be done in factories rain or shine, night or day.

The new systems were slow to take hold at first because workers resisted the enforced discipline that industrialization required. As factory owners realized the potential profit and cost advantages of the work, however, they offered workers little choice but to accept their new conditions. Unfortunately, those conditions were often unsafe or unsanitary. Accidents and disease were all too common. Until 1833, there were no laws limiting the use of child labor. Factory owners thought small children were ideal workers because they complained little and could access areas of machinery too small for adults. Children as young

Railways were one of several industries transformed during the Industrial Revolution.

as four years old were forced to work twelve-hour days until legislation was passed in 1833.[3]

The transition to factory systems also changed the face of British cities. Immigrants flooded major industrial cities like Liverpool and Manchester in search of employment. New railway lines began connecting even the smallest towns across the country. As a result, cities grew more and more overcrowded. Pollution from the factories' soot and smoke made the workers' living conditions dingy and unhealthy. While factory owners were earning huge amounts of money, uneven distribution of wealth saw only a fraction of the profits being returned to the workers themselves. Many were forced to live in terrible poverty in the already overpopulated cities.

The empire abroad played an interesting role in England's increased industrialization. Industrialization both benefited the empire and benefited from the empire. Increased technology, for example, helped make possible the colonization of other countries. Superior military technology made it easier for the British to conquer native peoples who did not have the same kinds of weapons. Industrialization also made access to foreign ports easier—shipping and communications time decreased dramatically. Profits from increased production provided money for further imperial expansion. At the same time, the empire provided new resources, which meant even greater profits for England. For example, raw cotton was harvested in India, shipped to the factories in

England, manufactured into textiles, and then exported and sold for profit. In other words, industrialization and imperialism were largely part of the same cycle in nineteenth-century Britain.

Effects of Imperialism

The most immediate effect of increased imperial efforts—for mother England at least—was profit for Britain. Although Britain forced its own imperial will on other countries, the colonized did not necessarily express unhappiness at first. During the course of Victoria's rule, the exploitative nature of the relationship between colonized and colonizer became clearer. The practice of colonized people trying to break away from a mother country's control and promote their own country's self-interest is known generally as nationalism. Growing nationalist movements among British colonies were an issue England would have to revisit again and again during the course of Victoria's sixty-four-year reign.

Chapter 4

The Early Years of Victoria's Reign

The first few months and even years of Victoria's reign were a very happy time for the young queen. Victoria moved from Kensington Palace to the more elaborate Buckingham Palace. Her mother came with her, but the duchess was given separate quarters. Conroy also came to Victoria's court as one of the duchess's advisors. While Victoria granted him the decorative title of "baron," she otherwise had nothing to do with him.[1] For the first time in her life, Victoria enjoyed the freedom of being on her own. She was also very pleased with her new privileges as monarch, including jewels, clothes, priceless works of art, and a very large annual salary.

Victoria spent her days learning to attend to official business. Her evenings were often spent at parties where she danced until dawn. Her official

A portrait of a young Queen Victoria

coronation—the day she was crowned—in 1838 was the ultimate in these celebrations. The ceremony itself lasted for five hours. The entire time, Victoria wore rich robes and furs and a very heavy crown decorated with all types of jewels. The crown gave Victoria a headache, but she still went through the ceremony with grace.[2] The real entertainment began after the ceremony ended. For four days there were celebrations in the streets, fairs in the park, and fireworks at night throughout London.

Lord Melbourne and Parliament

Victoria was crowned queen at a time when the government in England was undergoing major changes. Power was gradually being transferred from the monarch to an elected governing body called Parliament. Victoria was lucky to find a mentor and friend in Lord Melbourne, the prime minister at the time she was crowned, to help her understand these changes.

During Victoria's reign, the monarch only made formal decisions based on the advice of her ministers. The prime minister was the head of this group. The ministers, in turn, were members of the main governmental branch of Parliament, the House of Commons. The House of Commons was elected by a portion of the general public. Prior to Victoria's reign, the monarch played a major role in determining who would be in the House of Commons and the House of Lords (the other House of Parliament). As a result, only men of a very high social class represented the public in Parliament. The middle and lower classes found this system unfair.

Before 1832, only upper-class white men had the right to vote. The Reform Act of 1832 granted voting rights to a small percentage of the general public for the first time. While definitely an improvement, the first Reform Act gave voting rights to only one in every five men.[3] Most working-class men, all women, and all people of color were still denied the vote. During the course of Victoria's reign, two other Reform Acts were passed—one in 1867 and one in 1884. These new acts meant voting power was gradually given to the male British public, making the election process more democratic.

The Reform Act of 1832 also transformed the process of choosing a prime minister. Rather than the monarch appointing one, whichever political party held the majority of seats in the House determined who the prime minister would be. In 1838, Lord Melbourne's party, the Whigs, had controlled the House for the last three years. The Whig party had been a major force behind the passage of the first Reform Act.

While Melbourne was a member of the Whigs, he was personally very conservative and usually chose to maintain things as they were. Victoria already aligned herself with the conservative Whig party's values and beliefs. Her relationship with Melbourne only served to strengthen that allegiance. Some people felt

Victoria's loyalty to Melbourne and his party was inappropriate since she often became too one-sided when considering political issues. Many people felt monarchs should not take sides and were unhappy with Victoria's obvious favoritism.

Melbourne, then fifty-eight, was calm, sensitive, and intelligent. He provided the young woman with a sense of comfort and strength as she made the transition from girl to queen. Victoria wrote of Melbourne in her diary, "I like him very much and feel confidence in him. He is a very straightforward, honest, clever and good man."[4] He met with Victoria daily to help her draft letters to and from the other ministers of state, and to attend to other official business. Often the pair spent over six hours a day working together.[5] The afternoons were usually spent together in horseback-riding parties, and they dined together in the evening. Melbourne served not only as a political mentor, but as a grandfather figure as well. In the short time he remained in Parliament, until 1841, Melbourne had a major influence on the young queen.

Scandals at Court

The first two years of her reign, Victoria enjoyed enormous public support. Her maturity and good taste set her apart from the extravagant monarchs before her. Beginning in 1839, however, Victoria saw her popularity decline, in large part due to two great scandals. First, in 1839, Victoria accused one of her mother's attendants, Lady Flora Hastings, of being pregnant and unwed.

Victoria had always been suspicious of Hastings, who was friends with Conroy. Victoria believed the pair was more than just friends. In writing about Hastings's supposed pregnancy, Victoria assumed that "the horrid cause of all this is the Monster and Demon Incarnate whose name I forbear to mention."[6] In other words, not only was Victoria accusing Hastings of being pregnant, but she was accusing Conroy of being the father.

Victoria based these charges on the fact that Lady Hastings's belly had begun to get larger as if she were expecting a baby. As it turned out, Hastings had a fatal cancerous tumor, which made her stomach swell. No longer demonstrating the maturity she had shown only a year earlier, Victoria refused to accept the truth or to apologize, even after doctors explained the situation. Victoria came across as very stubborn and unsympathetic, especially after Hastings died. The public did not admire her for her actions.

Later that year, a shift in Parliament forced Melbourne to resign as prime minister. Victoria was very upset at the thought of losing her friend and mentor. She was also unhappy with the new prime minister, Robert Peel—a member of the opposing Tory political party. Peel asked the queen to replace her Whig attendants with women from the majority's party, as was tradition. Victoria refused. She publicly stated that she did not want Tory morality, which she disagreed with, to reflect poorly on her as queen. Privately, though, Victoria hoped this step would be a means of bringing back Melbourne's ministry.

Surprisingly, Victoria's manipulations worked. Melbourne returned to Parliament for another two years. The "Bedchamber Crisis," as it came to be known, however, left both Victoria and Melbourne very unpopular in the eyes of the public. People were once again unhappy to see their queen act so stubbornly. They were disappointed in the favoritism that she showed toward one party.

Source Document

The state of agony, grief and despair into which this placed me may be easier imagined than described! All all my happiness gone! That happy peaceful life destroyed, that dearest, kind Lord Melbourne no more my minister . . . I said [Lord Melbourne] must come and see me . . . for I shall feel quite forsaken, at which he gave me such a look of grief and feeling, and was much affected. He said "God bless you, Ma'am, and kissed my hand . . . I was in a dreadful state of grief.[7]

Victoria's May 7, 1839, diary entry reveals how upset she was to learn Lord Melbourne was forced to resign as prime minister.

The Opium Wars

Around the time of the scandals at court, affairs abroad, particularly in the Far East, were also not casting the empire in a positive light. For centuries, China had worked to remain untouched from Western influence. In fact, in the earliest part of the nineteenth century, Western influence barely reached east beyond Calcutta, India.

As Europe, and Britain in particular, recognized the trade potential in the Far East, attempts to open China to foreign trade became more aggressive. Europeans were eager to get their hands on China's resources, such as teas, silks, and porcelain. The Chinese, however, had virtually no interest in any of Europe's manufactured goods. For Britain, the key to resolving this imbalance lay in the cultivation of opium. Opium is a drug obtained from poppy flower seeds that relieves tension and pain, but is also dangerously addictive. The plants grew abundantly in India, which Britain controlled. As a result, the British were able to create a profitable drug monopoly.

China recognized the dangers of opium and had passed laws banning the drug as early as 1729. The British chose to largely ignore these rules. They simply smuggled the drug into China, buying the in-demand goods with the profits. As the drug trafficking increased, so did Chinese addiction to the powerful drug. The widespread opium addictions caused major social and economic disruptions throughout the country.

This monument to Queen Victoria in Hong Kong symbolizes the increasing visibility of British influence in the Far East during her reign.

Beginning in 1839, the Chinese attempted to stop the illegal trade. The resulting series of conflicts became known as the Opium War. Hostilities lasted until 1842, when the British ultimately proved victorious. The Treaty of Nanking officially ended the war. The British were granted not only the right to effectively continue trading opium in China, but also control of five major seaports, including Shanghai. China also ceded the island of Hong Kong to Britain altogether. The Chinese were humiliated after their first major military clash with the West. They had lost trading privileges and territories in their own backyard.

While the Opium War proved very beneficial to the British, it ultimately represented imperialism at its worst. Essentially, the British were willing to ignore the widespread damage their encouragement of opium was having on the Chinese people in the name of their own profit.

Victoria's Marriage and Children

In Victoria's own life, a series of personal events in the 1840s proved more important than foreign affairs. These events included her marriage and the birth of several children.

Victoria was generally expected to marry by the time she was twenty. Unmarried women were known as "old maids" and were looked down upon by society. It was important that the queen get married early to avoid this label. For some time, Victoria's Uncle Leopold had been trying to arrange a match with her first cousin, Albert of Saxe-Coburg (a province in what is now Germany). In the nineteenth century, it was not unusual for royalty to marry within their own families.

While the cousins had met and spent time together on several occasions, neither felt particularly attracted to the other. Albert was not as fond of the socializing, ceremonies, and parties as Victoria was. He also realized that marrying the queen of England would mean that he would be removed from his homeland. In a large sense, Albert would also not be as powerful as his wife—an uncommon position for a man in the nineteenth century. Also, the last time Albert had seen Victoria was three years before she became queen, and therefore before the unpleasant scandals. For her part, Victoria worried that a husband would try to control her. She also had a great fear of childbearing and did not look forward to pregnancy.[8]

Only a day after the pair were reunited in early October 1839, however, Victoria wrote in her journal that "my heart is quite going."[9] After a short four-day courtship, Victoria decided to marry Albert. Due to her royal position, it was up to Victoria to propose to Albert, and not the other way around as was common in the day. While Albert was not quite as enthusiastic as Victoria, it would have been in bad taste to refuse the queen of England.[10] He therefore accepted her proposal. The royal couple wed a little over one year later, on February 10, 1841. The elaborate ceremony was held at Westminster Abbey, a famous church in London. Albert wore an official

Source Document

At about 1/2 [past] 12 I sent for Albert; he came to the Closet [Queen Victoria's private chamber] where I was alone, and after a few minutes I said to him, that I thought he must be aware why I wished [him] to come here, and that it would make me too happy if he would consent to what I wished (to marry me); we embraced each other over and over and over again, and he was so kind, so affectionate; Oh! To feel I was, and am, loved by such an Angel as Albert was too great delight to describe! he is perfection; perfection in every way—in beauty—in everything! I told him I was quite unworthy of him and kissed his dear hand—he said he would be very happy and was so kind and seemed so happy, that I really felt it was the happiest brightest moment in my life, which made up for all I had suffered and endured. Oh! How I adore and love him, I cannot say!! how I will strive to make him feel as little as possible the great sacrifice he has made; I told him it was a great sacrifice,—which he wouldn't allow . . . I feel the happiest of human beings.[11]

In this passage from her diary, Victoria expresses her love for Albert.

military uniform. Victoria, who walked down the aisle to the national anthem, wore a while satin gown trimmed with orange blossoms.

At first, Victoria was willing to share everything but power with her new husband. Many British citizens were unhappy with the idea of their queen being married to a foreigner. As a result, Victoria and her advisors thought it best that Albert not be involved in any political decisions.[12] In fact, at the beginning of their marriage, Victoria felt that, as queen, she should be making all the decisions for her husband. Albert was not pleased with this arrangement. He was furious, for example, to learn that Victoria had chosen all his personal servants for him without even consulting him first.[13] While Victoria and Albert may have loved each other, they found themselves frequently arguing over issues of power.

Within a year of their marriage, the couple had their first child, Princess Victoria Adelaide. While Victoria was a loving mother, she immensely disliked being pregnant and had terrible trouble giving birth. She often had uncontrolled temper outbursts and became very depressed during her pregnancies. Though she and Albert would go on to have eight more children, she always thought of childbearing as an unpleasant and unavoidable accompaniment to marriage. She was unhappy with the way pregnancy kept her from the activities she enjoyed, such as horseback riding and dancing. Her day-to-day duties as queen were also more difficult to perform.

Only three months after Vicky's birth, Victoria was dismayed to learn that she was again pregnant. In 1842, she gave birth to a son, Albert Edward. Victoria and Albert nicknamed him Bertie. As oldest male child, Bertie was "heir apparent," meaning he would one day inherit the throne and become king. The British public rejoiced at hearing the news of the birth of Victoria and Albert's first son and their future king.

Shortly after Bertie's birth, Victoria and Albert had their most serious quarrel to that point. Princess Vicky became very ill in 1842. The queen's childhood nurse, Louise Lehzen, still worked in the royal household as a nanny. She tended the queen's children and, along with James Clark, the royal doctor, oversaw Vicky's treatment.

Albert felt the pair was not doing a good job in treating his beloved daughter. When he shared his concerns with Victoria, the queen became upset. She took Lehzen's side over her husband's. The result was a huge argument. For once, Albert would not back down. To show Victoria the degree of his anger, he wrote his wife a dramatic note:

> Dr. Clark has mismanaged the child and poisoned her with calomel [a medicine] and you have starved her. I shall have nothing more to do with it; take the child away and do as you like and if she dies you will have it on your conscience.[14]

Victoria was so surprised by Albert's strong reaction that she agreed to his demand. The next day she wrote in her journal, "I am ready to submit to his wishes as I love him so dearly."[15] After many years of service, Lehzen was given a generous pension and sent back to her original home in Germany. Princess Vicky recovered soon after.

The argument marked a turning point in the couple's relationship. Victoria involved Albert in more and more of her decisions. She soon became increasingly devoted to her "Angel," as she called her husband, and came to depend on him to make all her decisions, from what bonnet she would wear to affairs of state.

Victoria and Albert were married inside Westminster Abbey on February 10, 1841.

As Melbourne left the political arena, Albert stepped in as Victoria's unofficial advisor. He would profoundly influence her personal habits, morals, and political decisions over the course of their marriage. Albert was even more conservative than Victoria. Nonetheless, he tried to teach her not to side too heavily with one political party as she had done during the Bedchamber Crisis. In large part, Albert was responsible for installing the strict sense of propriety, good manners, and dignity that has come to be associated with the Victorian Era. He also taught his wife the importance of hard work and orderliness if she wanted to make her presence known in the government.

Afghanistan and India

While arguments in the royal household took up much of the couple's attention in the early 1840s, there were several much more serious situations stirring abroad. In the Middle East, for example, Britain found itself standing up against the powerful Russian Empire. Land in and around India was desirable to many countries because of the trade possibilities it opened up. Britain had much power in the area because it controlled such a large amount of land there.

In the late 1830s, Afghanistan, the country west of India and a small empire in and of itself, asked British authorities in India for help. The Afghans wanted to claim the land between the borders of India and Afghanistan. The British refused because they wanted the land for themselves. Once Britain refused, the Afghans turned to Russia for help. The Russians agreed.

For some time, the British had been nervous about the powerful Russian Empire expanding its influence closer to India. They were unhappy to hear the Russians were aiding the Afghans. In an effort to end the new alliance, the British demanded a Russian representative be removed from the Afghan capital city of Kabul. When the Afghans refused, the British declared war and the First Afghan War (1839–1842) officially began.

For most of the war, the Afghans proved little match for the superior British forces. In the winter of 1841, however, a large troop of British soldiers attempting to take over Kabul were brutally beaten by Afghan troops. Only one man out of thousands lived to tell of the excessive violence and cruelty.[16] The Kabul massacre was one of the first major blows to the Second Empire's seemingly endless expansion. Within a year, the British were forced to leave the country altogether—a major defeat for what many considered the world's most powerful country.

The Irish Famine

From 1845 to 1848, a different kind of enemy was causing unheard of human devastation across Ireland. The Irish farming system for years had been dependant almost exclusively on the potato. Then a poor harvest was followed by a rapid-spreading fungus that destroyed three consecutive crops. The result was a

HARPER'S WEEKLY.

JOURNAL OF CIVILIZATION.

Vol. XXIV.—No. 1209.]   NEW YORK, SATURDAY, FEBRUARY 28, 1880.   [SINGLE COPIES TEN CENTS. $4.00 PER YEAR IN ADVANCE.

Entered according to Act of Congress, in the Year 1880, by Harper & Brothers, in the Office of the Librarian of Congress, at Washington.

THE HERALD FROM AMERICA.

---

*In this cartoon, Ireland looks to the United States for help during
the famine because of inadequate British relief.*

full-out crisis. More than 1.5 million Irish people died from starvation or related diseases. Nearly another 1.5 million emigrated to other countries, including the United States, to try and escape the four-year blight.[17] Often, however, conditions in their new homes were not much of an improvement over the poverty in Ireland.

The Act of Union of 1800 had declared that Ireland would fall directly under British rule. At the height of the famine, many assumed the British would provide the necessary aid since it governed Ireland. The British response to the famine, however, was wholly inadequate. The poverty level in Ireland was overwhelming even before the famine. Unfair property laws left most people with no escape from their harsh living conditions. What the country needed was large-scale efforts to help restimulate the troubled economy. The government in London, however, provided minimal help to aid in such efforts and provided only the barest of direct famine relief.

Victoria personally took little interest in the crisis. She chose instead to focus her attention that summer on plans to build a family summerhouse in Scotland. Her journal entries are strangely silent on the subject of the "potato famine," as it came to be known. The most Victoria did was to limit her household's daily intake of bread to one pound per person. She did not want to be seen wasting food when others had none.[18]

Tension had existed between Ireland and England for centuries, in part because of religious differences.

Prior to the sixteenth century, both countries were predominantly Catholic. In 1533, King Henry VIII formed the Church of England after the Catholic Church refused to grant him an annulment from his first marriage. (When a marriage is annulled, it is as if it never existed. Annulment is the only way for a Catholic to end a marriage in the eyes of the Church.) The Church of England, or Anglican Church, became the official church of Britain. From the 1550s onward, the Anglican Church and the British people in general, gradually adopted Protestant beliefs and practices. Ireland, however, remained predominantly Catholic. As Protestantism in England grew, so did anti-Catholic, and consequently anti-Irish, sentiments.

By the time Victoria became queen, anti-Catholic feelings still raged throughout the British public. Many British citizens looked down on the Catholic Irish, even though they, too, were subjects of the same queen. The overall failure of the British government to react to the potato famine only added to the complicated tensions between the two countries. As anti-British sentiments increased in Ireland, so did feelings of Irish nationalism and a desire for independence.

New Zealand

Far away in the farthest corners of the empire, in New Zealand, more native peoples were voicing their unhappiness with the direction of British rule. British explorer James Cook had set his sights on New Zealand as early as 1769. For the most part, though, the British largely ignored the islands. In the beginning of the nineteenth century, missionaries began traveling to New Zealand in an effort to "civilize" the native Maoris, who were cannibals.[19] Missionaries were groups of individuals commissioned by a religious organization to convert those who did not belong to the same faith. In the case of New Zealand, missionaries believed it their duty to bring Christianity and Western education to the native people.

By the late 1830s, the missionary activities in New Zealand were taken over by the British government. The government wanted to bring the island under crown rule and encourage white settlement there. The Polynesian Maoris, however, were obviously not happy at the idea of their land being stolen from them.

In 1840, the British signed an agreement with fifty Maori chiefs that would bring the island under British rule. The Maoris would still be able to keep their land. Within only a year, though, the British were creating other agreements that ignored the terms of the original treaty. The Maoris began to rebel and, for five years, several skirmishes took place between the natives and the white settlers. Peace was finally restored in 1846, but only after the British honored their original agreement and made efforts to respect the needs and wishes of the native peoples.

Revolutions of 1848

The rebellions going on throughout the British Empire were actually quite minor in comparison to the full-out revolutions occurring all over Europe. In France, for example, revolution was brewing. The French people violently overthrew the corrupt government of King Louis Philippe in February 1848. News of the events in Paris inspired revolutionaries from Italy, Hungary, Bohemia, and Croatia all to wage various battles against the powerful Austrian Empire. Similar protests and rebellions also took place in parts of Germany.

Victoria was very upset at these events. She personally knew several of the displaced European monarchs. In fact, many of them found temporary refuge at Buckingham Palace after they were driven from their own countries.[20] The year of the revolutions she wrote in her journal: "It seems as if the whole face of Europe were changing. . . . I maintain that Revolutions are always bad for the country and the cause of untold misery to the people."[21]

While Britain was not directly involved in any of these conflicts, it did offer diplomatic advice. The British hoped this advice would protect their own foreign markets and help maintain a stable balance of power in Europe. These counseling missions were overseen by Foreign Secretary Lord Palmerston. Palmerston held this position several times over his lengthy political career, from 1830 to 1834, 1835 to 1841, and again from 1846 to 1851. During each of his terms as foreign secretary, Palmerston aggressively promoted British national interests through imperial expansion.

Palmerston took a relatively liberal viewpoint on the revolutions. He argued in some cases that the revolutionaries should not be stopped in order to prevent unnecessary violence. He advised the Austrian Emperor, for example, to compromise with his unhappy subjects in Italy and Hungary instead of fighting them. This advice, however, was largely ignored.[22]

Unlike most foreign secretaries, Palmerston chose to act without consulting the queen. This behavior annoyed Victoria very much. When he wrote to the Austrian Emperor without first showing the correspondence to Victoria, as was customary, she immediately voiced her surprise and unhappiness that "Lord Palmerston should have left her uninformed of so important an event."[23] Victoria was constantly writing to Prime Minister John Russell to ask that Palmerston be replaced as foreign secretary. Her correspondence from this period is filled with complaints against Palmerston. "The Queen must say she is afraid that she will have no peace of mind and there will be no end of troubles so long as Lord Palmerston is at the head of the Foreign Office."[24] Eventually Victoria's strategy worked. Prime Minister Russell forced Palmerston to resign as foreign secretary toward the end of 1851.

The Chartist Movement

London faced a small crisis of its own in 1848, although not a full-out revolution. Throughout the

1830s and 1840s, the British working class had been organizing to petition Parliament for various social and economic reforms. The movement was known as Chartism. Chartists were so called because their demands were presented to Parliament in a petition, or "People's Charter." The six main issues for which the Chartists campaigned over the years were: the right to vote, equal electoral districts, abolition of a law that required members of Parliament to own land, payment for members of Parliament, annual elections, and a secret ballot.

The Chartists had been relatively quiet the year or two before the revolutions in Europe. By 1848, however, Britain was facing an economic depression. Thousands of workers were left unemployed. News of the overthrow of the French government encouraged already agitated British Chartists to revive their movement. They planned a massive meeting to be held at Kennington Common in London on April 10.

No one had any idea how many demonstrators would arrive. The British government was in a state of great alarm. A similar gathering had brought down the French monarchy, and the British wanted to guard against the same fate. Military and police were put on full alert. Two hundred thousand citizens volunteered as special constables.[25]

As a safeguard, it was decided Victoria should leave the capital before the meeting. Victoria had just recently given birth to her daughter Louise Caroline. Even so, the queen was hesitant to leave for fear that her subjects would think her a coward.[26] In the end, Albert and the queen's advisors convinced her otherwise. On April 8, she and the royal family left for their home on the Isle of Wight, off the southern coast of England.

On the morning of April 10, processions of Chartists made their way to Kennington from all over London. The protesters marched and gave speeches throughout the morning. They were not unruly as expected, but rather demonstrated in a peaceful and orderly manner. The British officials had expected a mob of hundreds of thousands of Chartists. Only fifteen or twenty thousand showed.[27] By noon, drenching rain dispersed the crowd entirely.

The queen was greatly relieved to hear the march did not end in violence. The next day she wrote, "Thank God! The Chartist Meeting and Procession had turned out a complete failure."[28] Victoria was so quick to rejoice at the news that she never took the time to consider seriously the workers' petition. Many of their grievances were legitimate, such as the fact that they did not have the right to vote. For the most part, their requests were seen as threats to an overly cautious government and went largely unheard. The march at Kennington in 1848 was the last great Chartist movement. After decades of having their demands ignored by Parliament, as well as by the middle and upper classes, the Chartist movement fizzled completely shortly after the 1848 demonstrations.

On one hand, Victoria's reactions during the revolutions were understandable given her position. At the same time, she may have been responding out of fear and anxiety. Monarchies were being taken down all over Europe. As many of the exiled monarchs fled to Britain, Victoria saw them firsthand. For perhaps the first time, she was forced to think about the possibility that she, too, might not be queen forever. With all these uncertainties in the air, it was unclear what kind of world the looming mid-century mark would bring.

Chapter 5

The Victorian Age

Despite the revolutions of 1848, mid-century arrived on a personal high note for Victoria and her family. By 1850, peace had more or less been restored to the continent. England was once again a world leader in industry and political stability. With the scandals of her early years far behind her, Victoria and her family emerged at mid-century as the picture of domestic peacefulness. Queen Victoria was becoming more than monarch. She was a symbol of an entire era. As writer Lytton Strachey would later write, "The Victorian Age was in full swing."[1]

The Great Exhibition of 1851

Mid-century Victorian Britain was a time of great cultural and technological innovations. For some time, Albert had taken a personal interest in these particular areas. With the help of a committee and the approval of Parliament, Albert decided to organize an elaborate exhibit to celebrate the arts, sciences, and industry of the period. Nations from all over the world would be invited to exhibit. Of course, as the well-established "workshop of the world," the Great Exhibition would offer Britain a chance to show off its industrial supremacy and prosperity.

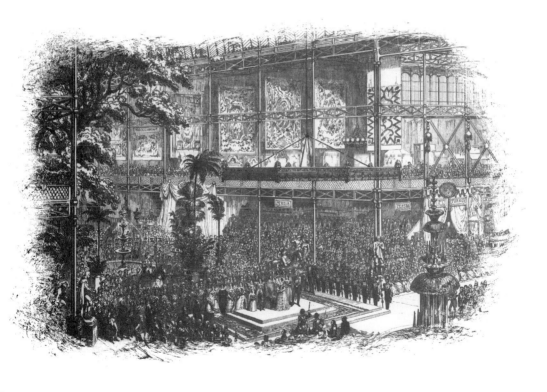

The Great Exhibition of 1851 was a triumph for both Britain and Prince Albert.

The centerpiece of the event was an enormous glass building. This "Crystal Palace" was built in Hyde Park and designed by Joseph Paxton. The greenhouse-like structure housed all the exhibits. Inside, over thirteen thousand exhibitors—at least half of whom were from Britain or its colonies—offered visitors glimpses at everything from locomotives to telegraphs to sculptures to a 186-carat diamond from India.[2] From the day it first opened on May 1, 1851, the Great Exhibition was a huge success. Over 6 million people would pass through the doors of the Crystal Palace in the six months it was opened. The exhibit generated a large sum of money, which was later used to build a permanent national museum.

Albert had always felt a bit of an outsider in his adopted homeland. He was, after all, a foreigner who married into the most visible family in the country. At times he was even unpopular for being born a foreigner. The overwhelmingly positive response to his idea was one of the first times he was embraced by the British public.

Victoria was very happy at the recognition the exhibition brought to both her husband and her country. She would later write that the opening of the Great Exhibition was "one of the greatest and most glorious days of our lives, with which, to my pride and joy the name of my dearly beloved Albert is forever associated!"[3] On the night of the opening ceremonies, she detailed the day's events in her journal:

The sight as we came to the centre where the steps and chair (on which I did not sit) was placed, facing the beautiful crystal fountain was magic and impressive. The tremendous cheering, the joy expressed in every face, the vastness of the building, with all its decorations and exhibits, the sound of the organ (with 200 instruments and 600 voices, which seemed nothing), and my beloved Husband the creator of this great "Peace Festival," uniting the industry and art of all nations of the earth, all this, was indeed moving, and a day to live forever. God bless my dearest Albert, and my dear Country which has shown itself so great today.[4]

For Victoria and millions of her proud subjects, the Great Exhibition was a monument to their own cultural and technological achievements.

Victorian Literature and Culture

Pinpointing the industrial advances of the age is easy to do, but what exactly was the Victorian culture embodied by the Great Exhibition? There is, of course, no single answer as to what makes up any culture. Even so, a general image of the Victorian Age began to emerge in the public imagination of the 1850s and onward. Today, the term "Victorian" brings to mind images of being proper and dignified. Victoria and her court were prime examples of this kind of etiquette.

The idea of "the home" and the ideal family were sacred to the Victorians. Again, many took the queen to be the picture of what family life should be. In reality, it is strange to think of holding up Victoria as the ideal mother since she so disliked being pregnant and giving birth. While she certainly loved her children, she did not really enjoy newborn infants in general either. In a letter to her daughter Vicky, the queen wrote that "an ugly baby is a very nasty object— and the prettiest is frightful when undressed—till about four months; in short as long as they have their big body and little limbs and that terrible frog-like action."[5] Victoria was also afforded power and authority that most women—who were expected to be only wives, mother, and homemakers—could never dream of. The "perfect family" was also an image that applied to white upper- and middle-class families. Poorer families living in slums or as colonial subjects were not granted such luxuries.

The paradoxes of Victorian life—the ideal versus the real—was a theme often explored in popular literature. Charles Dickens was far and away the most popular author of mid-nineteenth-century Britain. In books such as *Oliver Twist, Bleak House,* and *Hard Times,* Dickens brought attention to social injustices. Some of the subjects focused on included the working conditions in factories, the living conditions of the poor in big cities, and corruption of government. Women writers such as Charlotte Brontë and, later, Mary Ann Evans (who wrote under the name "George Eliot") critiqued the limited opportunities women had in society. Both women experienced such prejudice firsthand. They were both forced to write under male pseudonyms—false names—in order to have their work published.

Charles Dickens was the most popular British novelist of the mid Victorian Age.

Source Document

It was a town of red brick, or of brick that would have been red if the smoke and ashes had allowed it; but as matters stood, it was a town of unnatural red and black like the painted face of a savage. It was a town of machinery and tall chimneys, out of which interminable serpents of smoke trailed themselves for ever and ever, and never got uncoiled. It had a black canal in it, and a river that ran purple with ill-smelling dye, and vast piles of building full of windows where there was a rattling and a trembling all day long, and where the piston of the steam-engine worked monotonously up and down, like the head of an elephant in a state of melancholy madness. It contained several large streets all very like one another, and many small streets still more like one another, inhabited by people equally like one another, who all went in and out at the same hours, with the same sound upon the same pavements, to do the same work, and to whom every day was the same as yesterday and tomorrow, and every year the counterpart of the last and the next.[6]

Charles Dickens's best-selling novel Hard Times *details the living and working conditions in the fictional factory town of Coketown.*

The celebration of all things Victorian was followed by an increase in public interest in the empire abroad. This shift was due in large part to the major international events of the 1850s: the Crimean War and the Sepoy Rebellion in India.

The Crimean War

The British had always been concerned about the expansion of the Russian Empire near their prized Far East colonies, as was evident from their participation in the Afghan Wars a decade earlier. By the early 1850s, both British and French officials grew more and more uneasy with Russian influence in the area, particularly in Turkey. While Turkey was a small and relatively weak country, Britain took a great interest in it because of its geographical location. Turkey served as a buffer between powerful Russia and Western Europe.

The Crimea region is a peninsula—a body of land surrounded by water on three sides—on the north coast of the Black Sea. Today, the region is part of Ukraine. The events in this strategic area received great attention in the British media in the 1850s. As a result, public opinion began to influence the actions of the government. In 1853, for example, many British citizens were outraged to learn the Russians had sunk several Turkish ships in an unprovoked attack on Sinope Harbor.

When news of the attack on Sinope Harbor reached Victoria's old enemy Lord Palmerston, he enthusiastically advocated joining the war to fight against the Russians. While Victoria had seen that Palmerston was stripped of his foreign secretary title back in 1851, she was not wholly free of him. In 1853, he was still a very vocal member of Parliament. The British public became caught up in Palmerston's and others' propaganda. Soon war fever was sweeping the country.

At the same time, Prince Albert did not think going to war a wise decision and advised Victoria accordingly. Albert had always been against military action as a solution to conflict. He also realized that sending the unprepared British military to fight could end in disaster—after all, it had been many years since England had been involved in an all-out war.[7] The public, though, was crying out for war. They saw Albert's actions as unpatriotic and criticized his influence over their queen. Several of the smaller newspapers, to boost their circulation, began running articles that criticized Albert's influence over Victoria. The reports soon evolved into outright rumors. One paper even falsely claimed that Albert was a Russian spy working against the British government.[8]

Victoria was furious at the attacks in the press on her husband.[9] Despite Albert's advice, though, Victoria was eventually convinced to use military force. In February 1854, she wrote, "War is, I fear, quite inevitable."[10] A month later, Britain sided with France and the Turks to declare war against Russia. Although the queen had hoped war could be avoided, she threw her full support behind her troops once fighting began. In October 1854, she wrote, "I feel so proud of my dear noble Troops, who, they say, bear their privations and the sad disease which still haunts them, with such courage and good humour."[11]

As is often the case, the idea of a glorious war that captured the public imagination was a far cry from the reality in Crimea. The fighting during the course of the two-year war did not go well. Poor planning and bad commands left many soldiers unnecessarily dead. In the Battle of Balaklava, for example, a misunderstanding of orders led a large troop of British cavalry soldiers straight into the Russian line of fire. Only 195 out of 673 men survived the charge.[12] The battle was later made famous by poet Alfred, Lord Tennyson in "The Charge of the Light Brigade." A lack of supplies left the British troops dangerously low on food, clothing, medicine, and ammunition. Conditions in military hospitals were also horrible. Hundreds of men died due to poor medical treatment. Florence Nightingale, founder of modern professional nursing, responded to this crisis by organizing a government-appointed group of nurses to go to the front lines. With her help, the death rate in military hospitals was drastically reduced.

The Russians were ultimately defeated by 1856, but not without great cost to both sides. The British public and government had once cheered for war and dreamed of glory. By the end of the war, many were forced to recognize the massive suffering caused

Famous English nurse Florence Nightingale dramatically improved conditions in military hospitals during the Crimean War.

by the badly planned war. Many historians today consider the Crimean War in general to have been largely unnecessary.[13]

The Sepoy Rebellion

Soon after the end of the Crimean War, reports of other violence in the same part of the world began making their way back to Britain. In May 1857, British newspapers began reporting on an uprising of Indian soldiers outside of Delhi. Muslim and Hindu soldiers, known as sepoys, made up a large percentage of the East India Company's army.

Christian missionary activities and social, economic, and political changes brought on by British rule made the sepoys unhappy. The sepoys were also upset with how little regard the British had for Indian culture and religion. The breaking point came when the East India Company required the Indian troops to use a new kind of rifle. To load the rifles, soldiers had to bite off the end of a cartridge that was rumored to be greased with pork or beef fat. Hindus do not eat beef, and Muslims do not eat pork. Loading the new gun, then, forced the sepoy troops to break from their strict religious beliefs.[14]

In 1857, the sepoy troops rebelled against the British. The attack was unexpected and spread quickly to other areas of northern India. The British were taken by complete surprise. Since the military there was made up largely of sepoys, the British lacked the additional forces needed to fight back. Many considered the degree of violence and the high number of casualties on both sides to be even more shocking. The British public was appalled to learn that women and children were being slaughtered in the attacks. For Victoria, the death of British civilians was simply unacceptable.

While the British public was desperate for news from India, it took nearly six to seven weeks for reports to make their way back to England.[15] With a

Indian troops took the British military by surprise during the Sepoy Rebellion.

Source Document

We are in sad anxiety about India, which engrosses all our attention. Troops cannot be raised fast or largely enough. And the horrors committed on the poor ladies—women and children—are unknown in these ages, and make one's blood run cold. Altogether, the whole is so much more distressing than the Crimea—where there was glory and honourable warfare, and where the poor women and children were safe. Then the distance and the difficulty of communication is such an additional suffering to us all. I know you will feel much for us all.[16]

In this 1857 letter to her uncle, King Leopold of Belgium, Victoria describes her anxiety over the Sepoy Rebellion, particularly in terms of the deaths of British civilians.

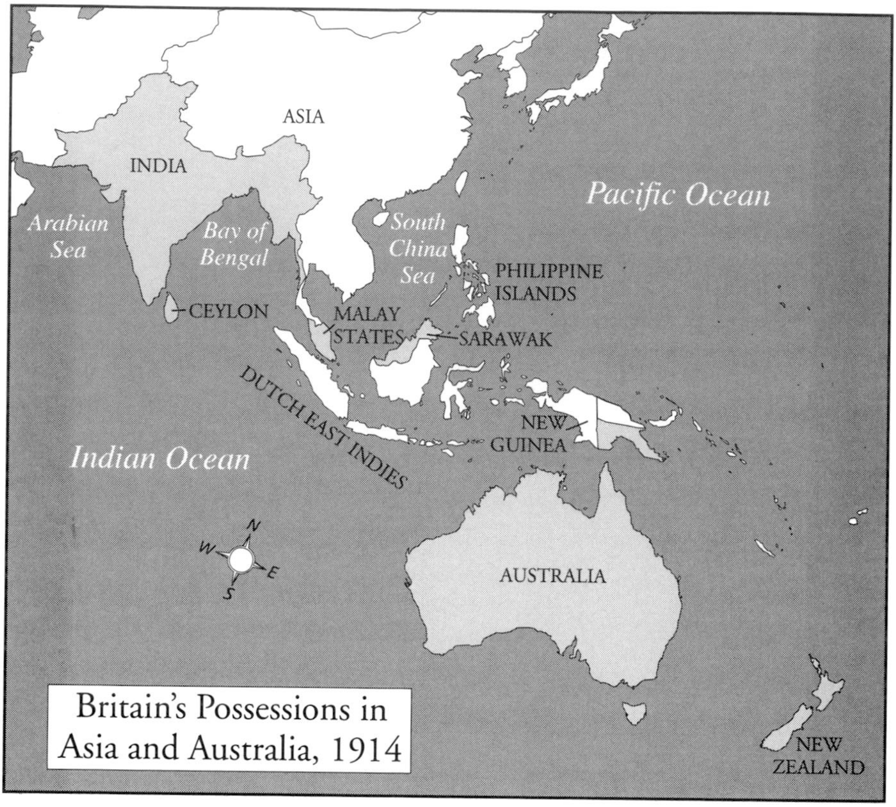
ASIA
INDIA
Pacific Ocean
Arabian Sea
Bay of Bengal
South China Sea
PHILIPPINE ISLANDS
CEYLON
MALAY STATES
SARAWAK
DUTCH EAST INDIES
NEW GUINEA
Indian Ocean
N
W
E
S
AUSTRALIA
Britain's Possessions in Asia and Australia, 1914
NEW ZEALAND

By 1914, Britain's Empire (shaded) would reach far into Asia and Australia.

lack of reliable stories, some newspapers resorted to printing rumors. Some of the stories trickling back to Britain were exaggerated or totally false, making the situation seem worse than it already was.

Shocking as the violent rebellion itself was, British retaliations were even worse. Those associated with the rebellion were tortured beyond belief, hacked to pieces, and even blown out of canons.[17] Whole villages were burned to the ground, sending more innocent victims to their graves. Once again, Victoria was concerned with civilian deaths. She wrote to one British official that she hoped "great forbearance is shown towards the innocent and that women and children will not be touched by Christian soldiers."[18]

Once the rebellion was put down, British officials decided a change in governance was necessary to avoid future conflicts. The East India Company, which had ruled for the British since its charter was granted in 1600, was dissolved. All its authority, military forces, and territories were taken over directly by the British government. That change, however, did little to fix the deep rift that now existed between colonizer and colonized. Although Victoria personally vowed to rule India in the best interest of all its people, the damage was already done. The tension between Britain and India would never really be lifted.

The *Trent* Affair

Not all foreign affairs during the middle years of Victoria's reign ended in violence. In 1861, for example, Britain avoided military conflict with the United States, due in large part to the diplomatic efforts of Prince Albert.

One of the primary causes of the American Civil War was the heated disagreement between the North and South over the issue of slavery. The Northern states did not rely on slavery because their economy was based on trade and industry. The North abolished slavery and many Northerners urged the South to do the same. The largely agricultural South, however, used slaves to work its huge cotton and tobacco plantations. The Southerners, then, were unwilling to give up slavery. As tensions continued to mount, the South eventually left, or seceded from, the United States in 1861.

When the American Civil War broke out, both the North and the South hoped for Britain's support. Although the British government officially declared itself neutral, it tended to side with the cotton-producing South because of its own commercial interests. This support was somewhat surprising considering Britain had abolished slavery in 1833, declaring it morally wrong.

In 1861, two Southern representatives sailed to Europe from Havana, Cuba, aboard the British ship *Trent*. They hoped to garner support for their cause. The Northerners found out, intercepted the ship, and held the crew. The British were outraged to learn of this violation of international shipping laws. U.S. president Abraham Lincoln at first refused to

yield and release the ship. In response, the British government sent troops to Canada in preparation for war against the United States.

Prince Albert took counsel with British foreign secretary Lord John Russell shortly after the deployment of troops. He helped draft correspondence that was firm enough to demand a formal apology, but would not yet declare war.[19] The strategy apparently worked. President Lincoln apologized soon after and released the *Trent*. Many historians credit Albert with having eased the tense situation. He played a critical role in avoiding unnecessary violence. Victoria, as usual, was very proud of her husband's accomplishments.

A Distraught Queen

The *Trent* affair and all the events of 1861 were overshadowed for Victoria by personal tragedies. First, in March, her mother passed away. While the mother and daughter had always had a tense relationship, it was still a painful loss for the queen. It was the first time someone so close to her had died. In fact, Victoria later wrote that she had "never been near a coffin before" her mother's death.[20] Victoria relied heavily on Albert not only for emotional support, but to take care of many official duties during her depression.

Victoria and Albert's oldest son, Albert Edward, nicknamed Bertie, was another cause of stress. For years, the future king did little to live up to his royal status. The young man was far too fond of women, drinking, and gambling for his parents' taste. Victoria and Albert were concerned that their son would damage the dignified image they had worked to create for the British monarchy. They feared he might bring back the image of extravagance that King George IV had represented.

In hopes that the aimless young man would find his calling, Victoria and Albert sent Bertie on a tour of North America as an ambassador. Unfortunately, Bertie lived the wild life to the best of his ability while abroad. British newspapers soon began reporting on the prince's outrageous behavior. In 1861, the biggest scandal to that point became public knowledge, when stories of an affair between Bertie and an actress named Nellie Clifden made their way around London. Albert, in particular, was devastated to learn of his son's behavior. He wrote to Bertie in November 1861, "on a subject which has caused me the deepest pain I have yet felt in this life."[21] Bertie had little time to respond to his heartbroken father, however, as Albert fell ill only a few days later.

Albert had long been a hypochondriac—a person who always believes he or she is ill. He complained constantly about various ailments and, at the same time, was given to overworking. At first, many around him thought that his latest illness was not that serious and was a product of stress. Within a few days, however, Albert was feverish and at times even delirious. His doctors diagnosed him with typhoid fever. Victoria kept constant vigil over her beloved husband. In part, she blamed her son, convinced that the heartbreak his behavior brought Prince Albert caused the illness in the first place. In the end, there was little anyone could do. Prince Albert died on December 14, 1861.

The queen almost immediately sank into a deep depression, keeping herself from all public life. Albert had been a dominating force not only as her partner, but also as her political advisor. While only time would show the exact effects, it was clear from the beginning that his death would affect not only his widow, but Britain as well.

Chapter 6

The Race
for Empire

Albert's death was a turning point in Victoria's reign. She became increasingly secluded. She avoided most public appearances, except for the dedications of memorials in Albert's honor. Even at her son Bertie's marriage to Princess Alexandra of Denmark in 1863, Victoria watched the ceremonies from an isolated corner because she could not face the crowds. Victoria ordered that her husband's rooms be kept as if he were still alive, even staffing them with servants. Fresh clothes were laid out for him every day. She also took to wearing only black as a sign of her constant mourning. Victoria upheld this ritual for the rest of her life. Many of Victoria's subjects were concerned that she might be going insane.[1]

Much as Victoria may have wanted, time, of course, did not stand still outside the walls of the

After her husband's death, Victoria wore only all black for the rest of her life.

Source Document

What is to become of us all? Of the unhappy country, or Europe, of all? For you all, the loss of such a father is totally irreparable! I will do all I can to follow out all his wishes—to live for you all and for my duties. But how I, who leant on him for all and everything—without whom I did nothing, moved not a finger, arranged not a print or photograph, didn't put on a gown or bonnet if he didn't approve it shall be able to go on, to live, to move, to help myself in difficult moments? How I shall long to ask his advice! Oh! It is too, too weary![2]

In a letter to her daughter Vicky, Queen Victoria raises the question of how effective a monarch she will be without her beloved husband and advisor.

palace. Even with a queen in self-imposed exile, changes occurred in the last decades of the nineteenth century. Two years before Albert's death, for example, Charles Darwin set forth the radical notion of evolution in his book *On the Origin of Species*. After years of studying plant and animal wildlife, Darwin proposed that human beings, like all species, evolved from more primitive species through a process of natural

ON

THE ORIGIN OF SPECIES

BY MEANS OF NATURAL SELECTION,

OR THE

PRESERVATION OF FAVOURED RACES IN THE STRUGGLE
FOR LIFE.

By CHARLES DARWIN, M.A.,

FELLOW OF THE ROYAL, GEOLOGICAL, LINNÆAN, ETC., SOCIETIES;
AUTHOR OF 'JOURNAL OF RESEARCHES DURING H. M. S. BEAGLE'S VOYAGE
ROUND THE WORLD.'

LONDON:
JOHN MURRAY, ALBEMARLE STREET.
1859.

Charles Darwin revolutionized the study of biology and more with the publication of his book On the Origin of Species.

selection, or "survival of the fittest." Darwin's theory revolutionized biology and upset many firmly held religious beliefs.

From the 1860s on, society also witnessed an increase in organized feminist movements. Those interested in what was called "the Woman Question" fought for a variety of issues ranging from the political to the personal. Seemingly silly debates took place as to how low was too low for a neckline and what the appropriate undergarments were for riding bicycles. Other women campaigned for equal educational opportunities, financial independence, divorce and property law reform, access to safe birth control, and the right to vote. All in all, these issues combined to challenge the very notion of a woman as quiet, servile caretaker to husband and children.

Victoria, however, was dead set against the movement. Her antifeminism was surprising considering her own position of power. She firmly believed that men and women were destined to occupy separate social spheres. She not only opposed the women's rights movement, but felt that those involved "ought to get a good whipping."[3]

Love of Empire

Another sign of the times was a general interest in all things exotic. Fed by the press, the British public clamored for stories of the empire beyond the shores of their island nation. This renewed interest came at a time when government policies were helping expand the empire at an incredibly fast pace. In fact, from 1874 to 1902, Britain gained more than an additional 4.7 million square miles of territory and authority over an additional 90 million people.[4] Whereas earlier imperialist efforts were grounded primarily in the desire to create new markets, this new wave encouraged imperialism for its own sake. Colonies were a source of national pride and power. As rival countries such as France and Germany began claiming more land, Britain, too, flexed its imperial muscles in order to demonstrate its superiority. No other place on earth was more susceptible to this race to colonize than the continent of Africa.

Stanley and Livingstone

In 1871, reporter Henry Morton Stanley undertook a long trek through Africa in search of British explorer and missionary David Livingstone. (Missionaries try to convert people of other religions to their own.) The missionary was believed to be missing somewhere on the continent. Five years earlier, Livingstone had set off on an expedition to central Africa. He was attempting to discover the source of the Nile River, which was a question historians and geographers had puzzled over for centuries. No one had heard from Livingstone since he left in 1866.

Against all odds, Stanley made his way through central Africa to find the missionary. In fact, Livingstone was never really lost. Rather, he was ill, weak, and lacked the supplies to return home.

Even so, Stanley's account of "finding" Livingstone became an international sensation. Stanley's famous question—"Dr. Livingstone, I presume?"—became a catchphrase all over the world as newspapers reported on the meeting.

Before the meeting, European countries had merely maintained trading stations along the African coast. Raw materials such as rubber, cocoa, and palm oil were harvested in the name of commercial interests.[5] Missionaries also made their way to Africa, feeling it their Christian duty to "uplift" the supposedly uncivilized native peoples. Stanley and Livingstone's expedition, however, created an image of the sheer adventure of exploration. It also brought new attention to an area of the world most knew little about. In part, the public's fascination with the unknown helped Stanley's account of his quest became an instant best-seller. More importantly, the attention attracted to Africa helped set off a wave of colonialist efforts from across Europe and particularly from Britain.

Of course, the new attention was not necessarily good news for the Africans. On one hand, the Europeans brought with them new methods of transportation and communication, such as railways, roads, and telegraph lines. On the other, the Africans saw their land forcibly taken over for these purposes. The best land was stripped of its natural resources for the production of goods in Europe. Many farms were forced to grow profitable crops, such as coffee, instead

David Livingstone (pictured) had gone on many journeys into the African interior before his meeting with Henry Morton Stanley.

of necessary food crops. As a result, famine eventually increased dramatically in Africa. African customs and traditions were also disregarded as the colonizers enforced their own. All in all, the supposed benefits of European colonization seldom reached the Africans themselves.

Egypt and the Suez Canal

While Britain's trade to and from India was extremely profitable, it was not particularly convenient. To get to Bombay from London required a lengthy journey around the entire coast of Africa. A strategic waterway connecting the Red Sea to the Mediterranean could cut that journey nearly in half. In 1799, French emperor Napoleon Bonaparte commissioned a survey to see if such a passage was possible. Errors in the survey process mistakenly led the French to believe it could not be done. After two additional surveys in the early 1800s, the Suez Canal Company financed a new operation. Beginning in 1859, it started construction on what would become the Suez Canal. The Canal Company was granted a ninety-nine-year lease to operate the canal. The company, which was owned jointly by Egyptian and French investors, officially opened the canal in 1869.

At first, Britain was shut out from the profits the canal promised to generate. In 1875, however, an opportunity arose that Prime Minister Benjamin Disraeli could not pass up. The primary owner of the Egyptian shares of stock was bankrupt and looking to sell his portion of the company. Disraeli, of the Conservative party, seized the chance and arranged to purchase nearly half the controlling shares in Britain's name. Disraeli's actions were extremely irregular, though, because he never consulted Parliament and he borrowed the money against his own name.[6] Many politicians, particularly William Gladstone of the opposing Liberal party, criticized Disraeli for his decision.

In the end, however, the benefits to Britain of Disraeli's decision far outweighed any possible costs. Queen Victoria, who liked Disraeli a great deal, was not as upset with the prime minister's actions as she would have been with someone else's. In fact, she applauded his actions, admitting the purchase "was entirely the doing of Mr. Disraeli, who had *very large* ideas and *very lofty* views of the position this country should hold. His mind is so much greater, larger, and his apprehension of things great and small so much quicker than that of Mr. Gladstone."[7] Owning such a large percentage of the stock made the canal more accessible to British ships. In turn, shipping costs were reduced, profits increased, and communications between England and faraway colonies such as India and Australia were made faster. The hold in Egypt also offered Britain a strategic center in the Middle East.

Of course, the canal, which was located on Egyptian soil, was now operated solely by British and French powers. In 1881, Egyptian nationalists revolted against the government and the dual British/French influence. A shift in the British Parliament saw Gladstone replace Disraeli as prime minister. Unlike Disraeli, Gladstone was hesitant to become overly involved in Egyptian affairs. Even so, by now he understood the benefit of protecting British interest in the canal. Victoria, too, recognized that "Egypt is vital to [Britain]" and encouraged Gladstone to put down the rebellion as quickly as possible.[8]

Despite some political opposition, Gladstone dispatched military troops. The French eventually withdrew their forces from Egypt, leaving Britain to fight

The Suez Canal reduced the travel time between England and India by nearly 50 percent. Here, ships in the Mediterranean Sea wait to enter the canal at Port Said, Egypt.

alone.[9] Victoria continued to rally Gladstone. In February 1883, she wrote to him: "The Queen feels very anxious that nothing should be said to fetter or hamper our action in Egypt: we must have a firm hold on her *once for all*."[10] By 1883, the British had not only defeated the Egyptian forces, but had come to occupy the country completely. They would remain the controlling power in Egypt until the mid-twentieth century.

East and West Africa

Other British possessions in East Africa came to include Kenya, Uganda, Zanzibar, and Tanganyika (known today as Tanzania). In West Africa, Britain had maintained bases in Sierra Leone, Gambia, and the Gold Coast (known today as Ghana). British policy in this area was initially shaped not by commercial interests, but by humanitarian ones. British slave trade was outlawed in 1807, and slavery abolished in 1833, although other countries certainly continued the practices. The British believed their presence in West Africa would discourage other countries from the slave trade.

The last quarter of the century saw an increase in British interest in the area as competing countries, particularly France, carved out colonies of their own. In order to keep up with their competitors and to partake in the raw materials the continent offered, the British stepped up their imperialist activities in West Africa, capturing the Congo and the Niger regions.

Source Document

The geographical position of the East Coast lays it more within the general areas of our foreign policy than that of the West Coast. Our alternative route by the Cape to India may at any time make it important that we should have possessions of, or at least free access to, good harbours . . . and the large Indian trade which is there carried on . . . make it essential that we should secure a preponderating influence over its political future.

Commercially it has made great strides in the 10 years, which have elapsed since the Slave export was checked, and an impulse given to legitimate trade. Apart from the mineral wealth which is believed to exist between the coast and the great lakes, there is an unlimited capacity for the production of cattle, cereals, and all the usual articles of tropical trade.[11]

In this memorandum, a Foreign Office official highlights the importance of the African east coast in Britain's imperial plans.

For centuries before the Europeans arrived, African tribes had set up their own boundaries and borderlands. When Britain and other European countries divided up the continent, they ignored these tribal borders. As a result, warring tribes often found themselves forced to live side by side in the same colony. The intense conflicts between such rival tribes was, and remains, a major problem within the national borders European countries imposed.

South Africa and the Zulu War

After Egypt, the area most desirable on the African continent was the southern tip. The British had been given the Cape Colony of South Africa from France at the end of the Napoleonic Wars in 1814. However, Dutch settlers, known as Boers and later as Afrikaners, had settled there as early as 1652. In 1814, the Boers agreed to Britain's occupation of the colony in exchange for 6 million pounds. Many British citizens had since emigrated to the area.

The implications of the initial agreement were not well thought out. The British and the Boers disagreed over many issues such as land and military protection. The Boers, who were slave owners, also resented heavy British missionary activities in South Africa and were angry when slavery was outlawed completely in 1833. As a result, some Boers chose to leave the British-controlled Cape Colony and Natal, establishing the Republic of Transvaal and the Orange Free State in the process. Their emigration became known

Britain's Possessions
in Africa, 1914

*Despite some troubles during Victoria's reign, Britain would
still control vast amounts of land in Africa.*

as "The Great Trek." Even separate governments would not keep the Boers and the British from disagreements. Continually growing tensions would have far more serious repercussions later in the century.

In the late 1870s, however, Britain's larger problem in South Africa was with the native people. Well before any European settlers set foot in South Africa, the Zulu tribes had established colonies there. Unwilling to submit passively to the British occupation, Zulu king Cetshwayo organized an enormous army of tens of thousands. In 1879, the British Army demanded that Cetshwayo disband his troops. When he refused, the British attacked, thinking the Zulus would be no match for their advanced weaponry. The British severely underestimated the sheer number of Zulu troops. At the battle of Isadhlwana, the Zulus killed hundreds of British troops, taking British guns and ammunition with them. It was the worst defeat at the hand of a native army that the British had ever experienced.

Despite the crushing defeat, Victoria was certain that the British Army could fight back. She told Prime Minister Disraeli "not to be down hearted for a moment, but to show a bold front to the world."[12] Victoria's belief proved correct. Soon after the battle of Isadhlwana, Britain retaliated. Within six months of the initial conflict, they had defeated the Zulus and taken over their land as part of the South African colony. Despite the number of British troops that had been killed by Cetshwayo's men, Victoria requested

The Zulu warriors proved a greater threat to the British military than anticipated.

that the defeated Zulu king be treated well after his capture.[13]

Irish Home Rule

The general focus on Africa did not mean events in the rest of the empire were necessarily quiet. In fact, one of the primary debates from the 1880s onward had to do with "the Irish Question." The Irish had grown increasingly dissatisfied with British rule since the potato famine of the 1840s. Irish nationalists, led by Charles Stewart Parnell in the late nineteenth century, advocated the passage of "Home Rule" as a solution. Home Rule referred to constitutional reform that would reestablish a separate Irish Parliament. The proposed Irish legislature would have control over domestic affairs, but would still be subordinate to the armed forces, foreign policy, and trade of the British Parliament.

Many British opposed the proposed reform for fear that any kind of Irish self-governance might eventually lead to total independence and the breakup of part of the empire as a result. Prejudice also led many British to look down on the Irish as inferior. Among those uninformed people was the queen herself, who was appalled at "these dreadful Irish people" and believed them somehow incapable of governing themselves.[14] The bill was proposed and defeated multiple times. Some Irish reacted with acts of terrorism, including the bombing of several London buildings. Tension continued for years, as Ireland was not granted any autonomy until 1914.

Victoria and India

For Victoria, the colony of greatest personal interest was India. She became fascinated with what she perceived to be a mysterious foreign land. In Victoria's mind it was not a place of devastating poverty, but of wealthy maharajas—Indian royalty—women wrapped in saris—traditional Indian wrap dresses—and exotic animals. She even learned to speak a little Hindi and took to hiring several Indians as personal servants, despite the commotion the decision caused among some members of the royal court. In 1876, Parliament, under pressure from Prime Minister Disraeli, granted Victoria the title of "Empress of India." Victoria was thrilled and read stories of the extravagant ceremony in her honor that took place in Delhi, which she did not attend. From that year onward, Victoria took to signing her name "V.R.I.," short for the Latin *Victoria Regina et Imperatrix*, which means "Victoria Queen and Empress."

A Tale of Two Prime Ministers

Victoria's title was given to her thanks to the influence and advocacy of Benjamin Disraeli, prime minister in 1868 and again from 1874 to 1880. Disraeli's second administration marked the first time in nearly forty years that his Conservative party won majority in Parliament.

The Conservative party was a continuation of the old Tory party. They believed in upholding tradition and the existing state of affairs. In other words, conservatives chose to preserve the nation's institutions, such as the monarchy, the House of Lords, and the Church of England. Conservatives also felt it important to maintain the empire abroad. Economically, the Conservative party believed it was best for local governments and businesses to make their own decisions without the national government interfering. This economic policy is known as laissez-faire, from the French for "to let (people) do (as they choose)." Conservatives generally did not favor large-scale reform initiatives.

Like most conservatives, Disraeli was a great proponent of expanding the empire and, by extension, the power and prestige of Britain. For this and other reasons, Disraeli was a great ally of the queen and could do little wrong in her eyes. The move to grant her an ornamental new title was largely a political and diplomatic one. Actually, given the grumbling from the rest of Parliament, Disraeli would have gladly postponed presenting the bill to change the royal title. When he saw the queen was already too set on the idea to do so, he had little choice but to continue.

In opposition to Disraeli was Gladstone of the Liberal party. The Liberal party was an extension of the old Whig party. They generally supported many types of reform initiatives. Liberals advocated for the rights of individuals over large government. They believed more power should be given to the general public and the elected Parliament and less to the monarchy. In economics, they were proponents of free trade, which refers to the unrestricted international exchange of goods.

Gladstone served as prime minister four times between 1868 and 1894. As much as Victoria liked Disraeli, she disliked Gladstone. Like many liberals, Gladstone was an agent of many reform initiatives, most of which the queen opposed. Even the smallest of Gladstone's recommendations bothered the extremely conservative queen. For example, she agreed to the suggestion that the men in the British Navy be allowed to have beards, however, only on the condition that they not be allowed to have mustaches without also having beards.[15]

Gladstone also heavily criticized Disraeli's aggressive foreign and imperialist policies, which the queen supported. Unlike Disraeli, Gladstone went out of his way to keep the queen uninformed of any decisions of consequence to continue the trend of shifting power from the monarch to Parliament. This infuriated the queen. At times, she stubbornly disagreed with Gladstone just for the sake of doing so. Her popularity declined during this time as she often came across as spiteful and unreasonable.

The Eastern Question

One issue over which the three strong personalities clashed the most was the "Eastern Question"—a term used to describe the diplomatic problems in the former Ottoman Empire in the nineteenth century. The Ottoman Empire was a vast Muslim Turkish state that encompassed various parts of southeastern Europe, the Arab Middle East, and North Africa from the fourteenth to the nineteenth century. By the late nineteenth century, most of the Ottoman Empire had been disbanded.

While events had remained relatively quiet in and around Turkey, Afghanistan, and Russia since the Crimean War, reports of new violence began surfacing in the late 1870s. Power struggles between the many ethnic groups and religions in the region led the Turkish sultan, or leader, to try and forcefully suppress the "radicals" and Christians unhappy with his regime. Many European countries demanded that Turkey alter its unfair and abusive methods of government.

Britain, however, did not participate in the demands. Disraeli, who was prime minister at the time, felt it was not in Britain's best interest to do so. Gladstone, head of the opposing party, violently attacked Disraeli for his indifference toward those suffering at the hand of the sultan. He even wrote a pamphlet called "The Bulgarian Horrors and the Question of the East" to make his opinions on the subject more widely known.

Shortly afterward, the tide turned again, when Russia invaded Turkey. As the stronger force and the greater threat to commercial interests, Britain became more concerned with stopping Russia than Turkey.

Victoria still harbored anti-Russian sentiments from the Crimean War. She particularly insisted that Britain use force to stop the Russian advancement. Although motivated by different reasons, the queen for once agreed with Gladstone and not Disraeli. At her angriest she wrote, "Oh, if the Queen were a man, she would like to go and give those Russians, whose word one cannot believe, such a beating! We shall never be friends again till we have it out. This the Queen feels sure of."[16]

Source Document

The Queen must write to Lord Beaconsfield [Prime Minister Disraeli] again and with the greatest earnestness on the very critical state of affairs. From so many does she hear of the great anxiety evinced that the Government should take a firm, bold line. This delay—this uncertainty, by which, abroad, we are losing our prestige and our position, while Russia is advancing and will be before Constantinople in no time! Then the government will be fearfully blamed and the Queen so humiliated that she thinks she would abdicate [give up the throne] at once. Be bold![17]

In her typically overly dramatic fashion, Victoria demands more aggressive action against the Russians in this June 27, 1877, letter to Disraeli.

Disraeli, however, went against everyone's wishes by not engaging with Russia. He was convinced that the mere threat of force would be enough to force Russia to retreat. Although risky, his strategy eventually worked. As Russia withdrew from Turkey, both Victoria and Gladstone were forced to recognize Disraeli's diplomatic triumph.

Personal Crises

Victoria was clearly more agitated over the Russo-Turkish War than she had been about other foreign affairs in years. While she lobbied to make her opinion heard, it did not signal the beginning of a trend of renewed political involvement. For the most part, the late 1870s and early 1880s were a time of great sorrow for the queen. Various personal crises occupied a great deal of her energy. In 1878, for example, her daughter Alice died of diphtheria, a disease that infects the throat and affects breathing. The following year, the son of the empress and emperor of France, with whom Victoria was very close, died while fighting for Britain in the Zulu War. In 1881, Disraeli died, leaving Victoria to fend for herself against Gladstone's liberalism. Her close friend and personal servant John Brown passed away two years later. A failed assassination attempt, the seventh since she had become queen, took place in 1882 when a young man fired a pistol at her from only a few yards away. Finally, in 1884, her youngest son,

Prince Leopold, who had suffered since birth from the blood disease hemophilia, died at the age of thirty.

For years, the public saw the queen as a stodgy, old-fashioned figure, who refused to move ahead with modern times. Suffering so many tragedies in so little time, however, made Victoria a very sympathetic figure in the public eye. By the time of her Golden Jubilee in 1887, her popularity was at an all-time high.

Tension in South Africa

The discovery of diamonds in South Africa around 1870 brought many prospectors to the area. Among

Source Document

To-day is the day on which I have reigned longer, by a day, than any English sovereign, and the people wished to make all sorts of demonstrations, which I asked them not to do until I had completed the sixty years next June. But notwithstanding that this was made public in the papers, people of all kinds and ranks, from every part of the kingdom, sent congratulatory telegrams, and they kept coming in all day.[18]

On the day Victoria wrote this journal entry, September 23, 1896, she officially became the longest-reigning monarch in British history.

those were famous businessman and politician Cecil Rhodes. Rhodes became closely tied with the historical events of his adopted homeland. Later, in 1884, the discovery of gold in the Transvaal region brought even more fortune seekers. The Boers called these immigrants "Uitlanders," meaning "outsiders," and taxed them heavily. Under the Boer leadership of Paul Kruger, the government established policies that had the Uitlanders paying the vast majority of taxes, without granting them any political rights.

At the same time, Britain was still looking to assert its own influence. The South Africa Company, founded by Rhodes, was granted a charter to develop the area north of South Africa. This area later became Rhodesia, named after Rhodes, and today is known as Zimbabwe. Rhodes was an extremely wealthy and ambitious man, dedicated to expanding British domination in the area. His dream was to one day connect Cairo to the Cape Colony by railway, thus establishing a completely British-controlled coastline.

The British expansion, as exemplified by Rhodes, was in opposition to the Boers' plan. In 1895, Rhodes organized an uprising of Uitlanders, already unhappy at being taxed so heavily, to overthrow Kruger. The Jameson Raid, as it came to be known, was a miserable failure and served only to increase tensions. Four years later, the Boer War officially erupted.

Once again, Victoria and the British in general underestimated the abilities of their opponent. It took the professional and well-supplied British troops three

Tension between Dutch settlers, shown here, and British military in South Africa eventually led to the Boer War.

long years to defeat only sixty thousand amateur Boer soldiers.[19] Victoria did her best to keep up the spirits of the British troops. Despite being close to eighty, she knitted scarves and visited the wounded in military hospitals. During the 1899 Christmas season, she personally saw that the frontline troops received a gift of one hundred thousand tins of chocolate.[20]

While the British eventually defeated the Boers, Victoria would not live to see the war's end in 1902. The victory was costly, in terms of money, lives lost, and the negative impact on the image of the British Empire in general. All in all, it was an inglorious end to the final years of Victoria's reign.

Victoria's Final Years

Victoria suffered from many of the common ailments of old age from the time she was sixty onward. Declining eyesight made it difficult for her to read documents, so she sometimes had her servants or children read to her. Arthritis made walking difficult, and she grew increasingly reliant on a wheelchair as she moved into her seventies.

Despite these health problems, in 1897, at the age of seventy-eight, Victoria participated in her Diamond Jubilee—the sixtieth anniversary of her coronation. She showed as much gusto as she had during her Golden Jubilee ten years earlier. Although it was no doubt tiring, Victoria spent the day traveling the same six-mile route she had traveled back in 1837 when she was first crowned.

Celebrations for Victoria's Diamond Jubilee in 1897 were as grand as they were ten years earlier for her Golden Jubilee. Here, people and carriages crowd in front of the Bank of England and Royal Exchange during the Diamond Jubilee.

A few years after the Jubilee, however, Victoria's end was clearly near. For some time, her personal doctor had been concerned about the possibility of the queen having a stroke. On the morning of January 17, 1901, slurred speech, drooping facial muscles, and general incoherence confirmed his suspicions were correct. After a five-day struggle filled with sinking and rallying, the queen died. She was eighty-one years old.

Victoria's eldest son, Albert Edward, stepped immediately into the role of king. His first order of business was to oversee his mother's funeral arrangements. Per Victoria's request, several specified objects were placed with her in her coffin, including photographs, items of clothing, and a cast of her husband's hand. She was buried next to her husband in the Frogmore Royal Mausoleum at Windsor Castle.

Victoria had outlived not only her husband, but also three of her children (her son Alfred died a year before her) and several grandchildren. What's more, a large percentage of her subjects could not even remember a time when she had not been their queen. Victoria's death signaled quite literally the end of the era that bore her name.

Queen Victoria and the British Empire's Legacy

After Victoria's death, Albert Edward took on his new role of king with surprising dignity given his wild past. From the beginning of King Edward VII's reign, he worked to promote friendly relations throughout Europe. His role as a great diplomat and arbitrator of many international agreements earned him the nickname The Peacemaker. While Edward was a very popular monarch, he ruled for only nine years. He died in 1910 at the age of sixty-eight.

Victoria's personal legacy expanded beyond the English monarchy alone. Her children went on to marry royalty from all over Europe. Her eldest daughter, Vicky, for example, was the wife of the crown prince of Prussia and later became the mother of Emperor William II. Similarly, Albert Edward had married the princess of Denmark before he became

*Queen Victoria became a symbol of her nation and her empire by
the time of her death in 1901.*

king. Victoria's connections to so many royal families earned her the nickname Grandmother of Europe.

While the empire technically still grew between the years Edward reigned and the beginning of World War I in 1914, signs that British crown rule had run its course were beginning to unfold. By the end of the nineteenth century, several of Britain's larger colonies with substantial European populations, such as Canada and Australia, were allowed to manage their own governmental affairs. By 1907, these colonies and a few others were granted "dominion" status. Before World War I, it was not entirely clear what this term meant, although it was loosely defined as less direct involvement with the British government. Other regions that consisted of native peoples, such as those in India and Africa, were still seen as colonies of the empire and therefore under its rule.

In 1914, World War I broke out, pitting Europe's great empires against one another. When Britain declared war, it did so on behalf of the entire empire, including its dominions. By the time war ended in 1918, however, the dominions signed the peace treaties themselves and chose on their own to join the newly formed League of Nations. The League of Nations was a precursor to the present-day United Nations, which is a worldwide organization dedicated to international peace and security.

In 1931, the legislative authority of the dominions was made official by the Statute of Westminster. This loose organization of independent countries was known as the Commonwealth of Nations. Rather than pledging allegiance to the British crown, they came to recognize the monarch as a mere symbol of their association.

The remainder of the British Empire took longer to come by its independence. Nationalist movements developed quickly in places like India, Africa, and the West Indies during the years between World Wars I and II. Beginning in 1947 with India, Britain slowly began granting them their independence, with the option to join the Commonwealth. Mounting international pressure during the 1950s and 1960s influenced Britain to let go of its remaining colonies, many of which were in Africa. The last major British colony, Hong Kong, was returned to the Chinese in 1997 at the end of a ninety-nine-year lease.

While the British Empire has effectively been disbanded, its effects are still felt and will be for years to come. Perhaps the greatest contribution of the empire to its colonies was the technological infrastructure developed for the benefit of Britain's own commerce and administration. Much of the wiring, relay stations, railways, bridges, and water ports constructed in otherwise remote areas of the world, could have taken decades longer to be put in place had it not been for British Victorians.

On the downside, of course, British imperial policy exploited people, culture, and land for its own benefit. Many Victorians naively believed the empire existed to help "better" the peoples of the world who were thought incapable of governing themselves. This condescending theory was called the "white man's burden." For the most part, however, the vast amounts of wealth the empire generated for the mother country never reached the colonies themselves. Many colonies found themselves stripped of profitable natural resources after Britain's race to produce more goods. Britain's self-proclaimed cultural superiority also firmly fixed racist attitudes in many of the colonies and replaced the original culture, religion, and language with its own.

The British rarely set up long-term industries or provided training to their colonized subjects. This often left former colonies poorly prepared when finally granted independence. In some colonies, particularly in Africa, Britain did little to ease the transition to self-governance. The new governments at times established harsh dictatorships, which exploited the majority of their populations. Many of these varying and complex issues continue today to be problems in former British colonies.

The Victorian Age was not one single, simple, or unified era, only in part because Victoria's reign lasted so long. For good and bad, it was above all an age of change. The colonies and peoples that made up the empire were culturally and geographically a world apart. One of the few common bonds between places as far ranging as Ireland, Fiji, and India was Victoria herself. During the last third of her reign, she had become one of the most recognizable women in the world. Her image was plastered over everything from newspapers and magazines to mustard jars and postage stamps.

Ironically, while Victoria was the most beloved monarch in years, she achieved that recognition at a time when the power of the British monarch was steadily declining. By making the monarchy respectable again, Victoria guaranteed its continuance, ceremonial as the role would become. The oddly old-fashioned woman was also most popular at a time when her subjects were welcoming the advent of modernism. Rather than being criticized for being behind the times, however, Victoria was indulged for representing a time gone by. While Victoria may have been less and less directly involved in the political events of the day, she managed to restore dignity to the otherwise tarnished crown. She served as a symbol not only of domestic propriety, but also of a vast empire.

Timeline

1819—Alexandrina Victoria is born.

1832—First Reform Act passed, beginning a trend of increased parliamentary power and decreased power for the monarch.

1833—Great Britain abolishes slavery in its empire.

1837—Victoria becomes Queen of England.

1838
–1842—First Afghan War.

1839
–1842—Opium War with China.

1840—Victoria marries her cousin, Albert of Saxe-Coburg.

1845—Irish potato famine begins.

1848—Revolutions occur in Europe, although not in Britain; Last Chartist movement in London.

1851—Great Exhibition takes place in London.

1854
–1856—Crimean War.

1857—Sepoy Rebellion takes place outside Delhi, India.

1859—Charles Darwin publishes *On the Origin of Species*.

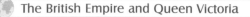

1861—U.S. Civil War begins; the *Trent* Affair causes a diplomatic crisis; Victoria's husband, Albert, dies of typhoid fever.

1871—Famous meeting between Henry Morton Stanley and David Livingstone in Africa.

1876—Victoria declared empress of India.

1878 **–1881**—Second Afghan War.

1879—Zulu War.

1881 **–1883**—War with Egypt; Britain wins and annexes the country.

1887—Golden Jubilee, fiftieth anniversary of Victoria's coronation.

1897—Diamond Jubilee celebrating Victoria's sixty years on the throne.

1899 **–1902**—Boer War.

1901—Victoria dies.

Chapter Notes

Chapter 1. The Golden Jubilee

1. Carolly Erickson, *Her Little Majesty: The Life of Queen Victoria* (New York: Simon & Schuster, 1997), p. 229.

2. Christopher Hibbert, *Queen Victoria in Her Letters and Journals: A Selection* (New York: Viking, 1985), p. 306.

3. Richard Hough, *Victoria and Albert* (New York: St. Martin's Press, 1996), p. 175.

4. Sally Mitchell, ed., *Victorian Britain: An Encyclopedia* (New York: Garland Publishing, 1988), p. 663.

5. Ibid., p. 263.

6. Ibid., p. 308.

Chapter 2. The Life of a Queen-to-Be

1. Carolly Erickson, *Her Little Majesty: The Life of Queen Victoria* (New York: Simon & Schuster, 1997), p. 7.

2. Christopher Hibbert, *Queen Victoria in Her Letters and Journals: A Selection* (New York: Viking, 1985), p. 9.

3. Richard Hough, *Victoria and Albert* (New York: St. Martin's Press, 1996), p. 21.

4. Erickson, p. 11.

5. Hough, p. 27.

6. Hibbert, p. 23.

Chapter 3. The British Empire

1. PBS Online, "Thomas Hutchinson and Loyalists," *The Liberty!: Chronicle of the Revolution,* 1997, <http://www.pbs.org/ktca/liberty/chronicle/hutchinson-loyalists.html> (January 22, 2002).

2. Sally Mitchell, ed., *Victorian Britain: An Encyclopedia* (New York: Garland Publishing, 1988), p. 280.

3. Ibid., p. 136.

Chapter 4. The Early Years of Victoria's Reign

1. Lytton Strachey, *Queen Victoria* (San Diego: Harcourt Brace & Company, 1921), p. 75.

2. Carolly Erickson, *Her Little Majesty: The Life of Queen Victoria* (New York: Simon & Schuster, 1997), p. 73.

3. Glenn Everett, "Reform Acts," *The Victorian Web,* 1987, <http://www.victorianweb.org/history/hist2.html> (January 18, 2002).

4. Christopher Hibbert, *Queen Victoria in Her Letters and Journals: A Selection* (New York: Viking, 1985), p. 23.

5. Erickson, p. 67.

6. Hibbert, p. 42.

7. Ibid., pp. 45–46.

8. Erickson, p. 83.

9. Hibbert, p. 56.

10. Erickson, p. 82.

11. Hibbert, p. 57.

12. Brenda Ralph Lewis, "The Love Story of Victoria and Albert," *Woman's History,* 2001, <http://womenshistory.about.com/library/prm/blvictoriaandalbert1.htm> (January 7, 2002).

13. Giles St. Aubyn, *Queen Victoria: A Portrait* (New York: Atheneum, 1992), p. 136.

14. Hibbert, p. 93.

15. Ibid., p. 94.

16. Erickson, p. 95.

17. Sally Mitchell, ed., *Victorian Britain: An Encyclopedia* (New York: Garland Publishing, 1988), p. 403.

18. Erickson, p. 117.

19. Mitchell, p. 540.

20. St. Aubyn, p. 243.

21. Hibbert, p. 76.

22. Mitchell, p. 573.

23. Hibbert, p. 78.

24. Ibid., p. 77.

25. Mitchell, p. 133.

26. Erickson, p. 110.

27. Ibid., pp. 110–111.

28. St. Aubyn, p. 223.

Chapter 5. The Victorian Age

1. Lytton Strachey, *Queen Victoria* (San Diego: Harcourt Brace & Company, 1921), p. 195.

2. Sally Mitchell, ed., *Victorian Britain: An Encyclopedia* (New York: Garland Publishing, 1988), p. 277.

3. Christopher Hibbert, *Queen Victoria in Her Letters and Journals: A Selection* (New York: Viking, 1985), p. 84.

4. Ibid.

5. Ibid., p. 112.

6. Charles Dickens, *Hard Times*, ed. Graham Law (Ontario: Broadview Literary Texts, 1996), p. 60.

7. Richard Hough, *Victoria and Albert* (New York: St. Martin's Press, 1996), p. 137.

8. Carolly Erickson, *Her Little Majesty: The Life of Queen Victoria* (New York: Simon & Schuster, 1997), p. 129.

9. Hibbert, p.123.

10. Ibid., p. 124.

11. Ibid., pp. 125–126.

12. Mitchell, p. 117.

13. Ibid., p. 202.

14. Hough, p. 146.

15. Erickson, p. 151.

16. Hibbert, p. 136.

17. Erickson, p. 152.

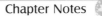

18. Hibbert, p. 138.

19. Hough, pp. 181–183.

20. Hibbert, p. 118.

21. Hough, p. 178.

Chapter 6. The Race for Empire

1. Richard Hough, *Victoria and Albert: Their Love and Their Tragedies* (London: Richard Cohen Books, 1996), p. 203.

2. Christopher Hibbert, *Queen Victoria in Her Letters and Journals: A Selection* (New York: Viking, 1985), pp. 156–157.

3. Carolly Erickson, *Her Little Majesty: The Life of Queen Victoria* (New York: Simon & Schuster, 1997), p. 198.

4. Graham D. Goodlad, *British Foreign and Imperial Policy, 1865–1919* (London: Routledge, 2000), p. 29.

5. Ibid., p. 32.

6. Giles St. Aubyn, *Queen Victoria: A Portrait* (New York: Atheneum, 1992), p. 433.

7. Ibid, p. 434.

8. George Earle Buckle, ed., *The Letters of Queen Victoria: A Selection from Her Majesty's Correspondence Between the Years 1862 and 1878,* vol. 3 (New York: Longmans, Green, and Co., 1907), p. 301.

9. Goodlad, p. 18.

10. Buckle, p. 407.

11. Goodlad, p. 37.

12. St. Aubyn, p. 439.

13. Ibid.

14. Hibbert, p. 267.

15. Lytton Strachey, *Queen Victoria* (San Diego: Harcourt Brace & Company, 1921), pp. 333–334.

16. Strachey, p. 362.

17. Hibbert, p. 245.

18. Ibid., p. 333.

19. Sally Mitchell, ed., *Victorian Britain: An Encyclopedia* (New York: Garland Publishing, 1988), p. 744.

20. St. Aubyn, p. 552.

Further Reading

Green, Robert. *Queen Victoria*. Danbury, Conn.: Franklin Watts, 1998.

Hibbert, Christopher. *Queen Victoria in Her Letters*. New York: Viking Penguin, 1985.

Lace, William W. *The British Empire: The End of Colonialism*. San Diego, Calif.: Lucent Books, 2000.

Myers, Walter Dean. *At Her Majesty's Request: An African Princess in Victorian England*. New York: Scholastic Press, 1999.

Netzley, Patricia D. *Queen Victoria*. Farmington Hills, Mich.: Gale Group, 1996.

Twist, Clint. *Stanley and Livingstone: Expeditions Through Africa*. Orlando, Fla.: Raintree Steck-Vaughn Publishers, 1995.

"The Official Web Site of the British Monarchy." n.d. <http://www.royal.gov.uk/output/Page1.asp>.

"The Victorian Web." n.d. <http://65.107.211.206/victov.html>.

"The British Empire." *British History*. 2002 <http://britishhistory.about.com/cs/britishempire/>.

Index